A LASTING

IMPRESSION

A History of Wheatons in Exeter

PATERNOSTER HOUSE
OLAND'S
K SILKS
SITE BROADGATE
NORTH St
HOLMAN, HAM
AND COMPANY
ESTABLISHED
1765.

A LASTING IMPRESSION

A History of Wheatons in Exeter

Anthony J Wheaton

A JW PUBLISHING

Dedication

To my forefathers who saw the opportunities and committed their efforts to make it all possible.

Acknowledgements

My sincere and loving thanks to my wife Annette for her patience in keying the text from my notes and drafts over six months since the suitcase was opened.

Thanks to my editor Clare Eastland who made sense of it all and particularly to my graphic designer Andy Jones of Topics – The Creative Partnership for his professional interpretation and layout.

Thanks also to the contributors, who worked for the company, for pictures of events and their recollections without which this project could not have been assembled.

Photograph on title verso (page 2):
Paternoster House, *185 Fore Street – destroyed by fire in 1882. It was from this shop that William Wheaton set up business in Exeter incorporating Mr Penny's bookshop founded in 1780.*

Photograph on page 6:
Exeter High Street in 1900. *Wheatons' book and stationery shop at 223 High Street is on the corner of Queen Street and High Street. In about 1927 the shop moved further up High Street to 231–232, just beyond the limit of this picture and on the left hand side of the street. Here, the shop was bombed and completely demolished in a World War II air raid in 1942.*

The 2017 first edition is published by
AJW Publishing

Highway House
Tedburn St Mary
Nr Exeter
Devon
EX 6 5AD
Great Britain

aj.wheaton@btinternet.com

ISBN 978-1-5272-1327-2

Edited by Clare Eastland.

Designed by Andy Jones,
Topics – The Creative Partnership
www.topicsdesign.co.uk

Printed and bound by Short Run Press, Exeter.

Note: *The founding directors of Short Run Press, Andy Gliddon and Murray Couch, were both employed in the production offices of A. Wheaton and Co. during the 1970s. Short Run Press is now managed by their sons.*

Preface

For 20 years a suitcase of family archives and Wheaton company records including pictures, newspaper cuttings, catalogues and memoirs assembled by my late father, John Wheaton, has been in my possession.

It is time to share selected contents and the events of later years with those who may be interested.

Having worked in the business for 27 years, including 20 years with Robert Maxwell after the Wheaton family sold the company in 1967, I have added further material to the collection. Most helpful material has been contributed by former colleagues and retired and working employees and their input has been invaluable in the preparation of this book.

This is not just the story of events at Wheatons and of those who worked there, many for much of their working lives, but also an account of the technical processes and practices involved. Labour intensive processes have largely passed into history in the mainstream printing trade, replaced by increasing automation and modern computer based technologies.

Wheatons has been one of Exeter's main industrial employers. Thousands of the city's people and families would have known someone who worked for the company over the years. Perhaps best known in the past for the bookshops in the city, the company became a significant employer through educational publishing, as stationers and as printers. In more recent times, the company expanded as book, journal and catalogue printers on the Marsh Barton Trading Estate under the ownership of Robert Maxwell's Pergamon Press. Later ownership passed to the British Printing & Communications Corporation (BPCC), the Polestar Group and finally a management buyout team.

This book is intended as a *'lasting impression'* of the company for ex-employees, my own family and those who may find the poignant story informative and interesting.

STATIONERS.
A.WHEATON &Co
QUEEN St

Contents

A type case tray with a compositor's stick

Background to the Wheaton Family

By the 1850s there were a number of Wheaton families farming in the Feniton and Fairmile districts of East Devon. They can be traced to seven farms in the area.

One family rented Cadhay House in 1895 and farmed nearby. Another family farmed at Whites and Downs in 1760. William Wheaton, the first printer in the family, was born here in 1790. (In 1840, when the new Exeter to London railway line cut through the farm it was sold off to a local landowner.)

In the days when the only mode of transport was the horse, travel would be limited to about five miles around. To find a wife involved travelling further to avoid inbreeding amongst country families. The first born son could expect to inherit the farm, others may need to find work elsewhere.

To emigrate to the colonies offered the promise of wider opportunities if one had a skill or a trade and was prepared for the risks. A sailing immigrant ship out of Bristol or Swansea could take eight to ten weeks to reach America.

Earlier, in 1636, Robert Wheaton was one of the first immigrants to Massachusetts, just 16 years after the Pilgrim Fathers arrived in North America. Over the years other Wheatons emigrated to America, Australia, Canada and South Africa on trading or immigrant ships. There are towns in America named Wheaton.

Fortunately, young William Wheaton stayed in Devon to train as a printer in Honiton. He would probably have lived in an attic in Honiton during the week as the six mile horse ride down lanes and tracks would have been an arduous journey.

Above left: *Cadhay House, near Honiton, Devon*
Above: *A piece of metal type*

William Wheaton, the Founder of the Company

Right: *Paternoster House, 185 Fore Street – destroyed by fire in 1882. It was from this shop that William Wheaton set up business in Exeter incorporating Mr Penny's bookshop founded in 1780.*

A Brief History of Wheatons in Exeter – the First 130 Years

The Wheatons company can trace nearly 200 years of continuous trading, originally as booksellers, educational publishers, book printers and commercial stationery providers. In more recent times the business evolved to provide technical typesetting, printing and binding services to scientific, academic and general publishers. Later this was to include short run scientific journals, timetables, directories, large pagination trade catalogues and commercial publications.

1835 William Wheaton, aged about 40, purchased an established bookshop business at 29 High Street, Exeter from a Mr Penny who had traded since 1780. William then launched Wheaton's Circulating Library and Patent Medicine Warehouse.

This was not William's first venture, however. Born at Larkbeare in East Devon, he had completed an apprenticeship with Honiton printer Spurway. In 1813, aged about 23, William with his wife Phoebe had purchased a bookshop and small printing business in Ringwood, Hampshire, with 500 guineas contributed by his mother. In about 1830 this business was left in the care of his son and daughter and William returned to Exeter.

1846 The Exeter bookshop by now operated from Paternoster House, 185 Fore Street, Exeter, with a small printing department printing chemists' labels, die stamping and engraving. Publishing commenced with local books including *The Exeter Almanack Compendium.*

An original copy of Wheatons' Exeter Almanac Compendium *from 1851. Sadly the cover has been lost*

A view of South Gate, Exeter. This reproduction is the earliest surviving item to bear the Wheaton imprint. This engraving was published in about 1838 not long after William Wheaton had acquired Mr Penny's business. Exeter was a walled city and this print shows one of the four main gates through which all traffic passed in and out. The print shows the city was already developed outside of the fortified city walls. The woman entering the gateway may well be carrying clothing washed in the river.

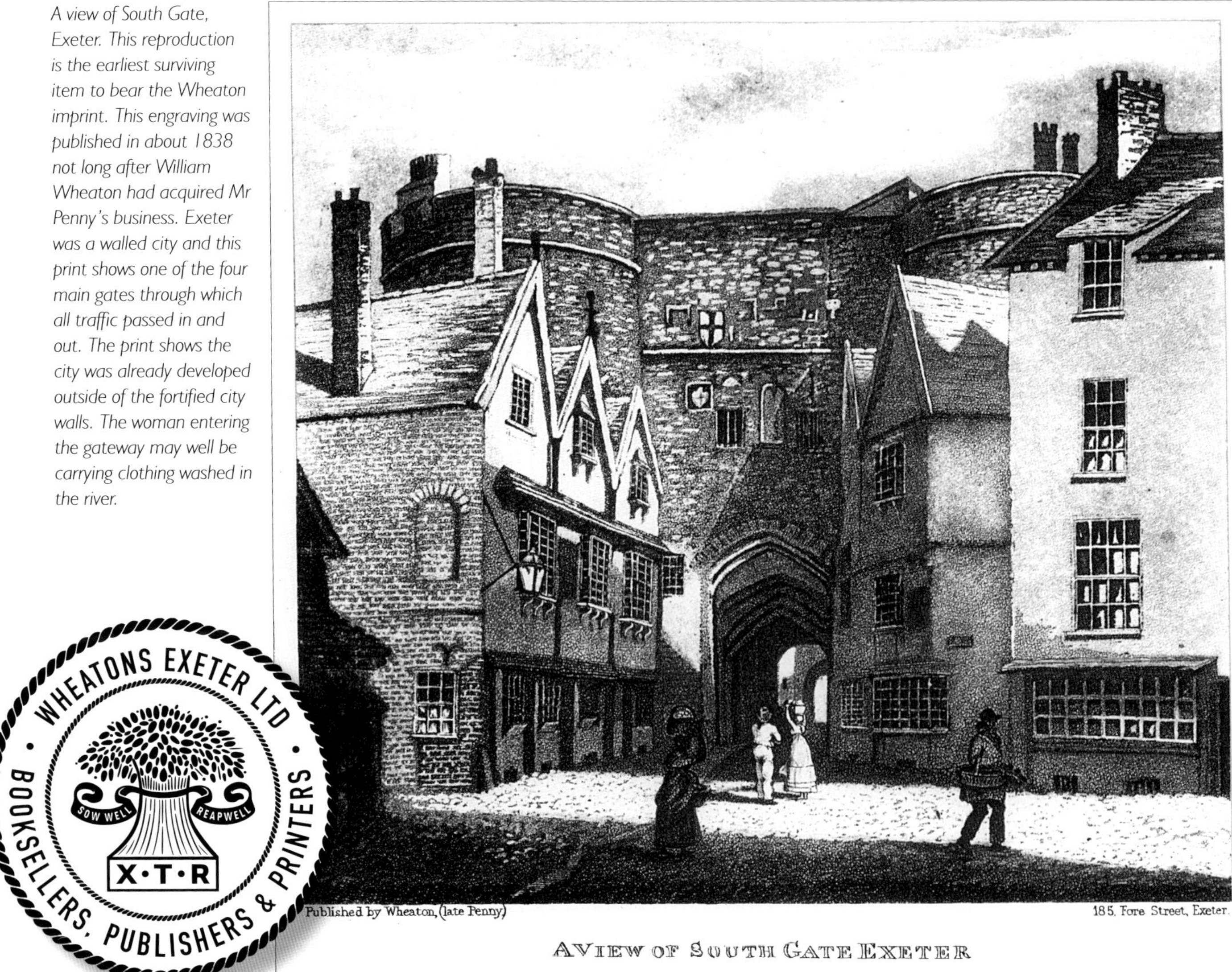

The first Wheatons logo

A drawing following the 'great fire of Exeter' in 1882 showing the destroyed buildings and the boarded up shop front of A Wheaton and Co.

1882–1900 In January 1882 Paternoster House, along with at least five adjacent shops and houses, was destroyed in 'the great fire of Exeter'. The bookshop and stationery business relocated to 223 High Street, Exeter (the corner of High Street and Queen Street) until 1905 or somewhat later.

When William retired the business was taken on by his son and daughter together with his nephew, Alfred, the Ringwood business having been sold in the late 1880s.

Most mornings Alfred would be seen standing outside his shop doorway welcoming people in from the pavement and thanking customers as they left.

1901–1906 During these years the company acquired Exeter printers Sidney Lee & Co of Preston Street, printers of labels, magazines and commercial print, in order to increase printing capacity.

Sidney Lee joined Wheatons as a factory manager. However, years later, in 1920, he gave the company one week's notice to leave the business and opened up a rival company of his own. He had connived to persuade some of Wheatons' customers to transfer their accounts to him. He also took with him three of Wheatons' foremen.

A new factory manager, Mr Hutt, was engaged from a printer near Bristol. He proved to be most capable and soon reinstated the foremen.

Sidney Lee & Co became re-established and continued to trade in Exeter as lithoprinters in premises in Water Lane until closing in the late 1980s.

1901–1914 Also acquired were several adjoining premises at 143 Fore Street, enabling the print works to expand into what had been the Western Times Company's newspaper publishing offices and print works. Built in 1714 by Exeter wool merchant Sir Thomas Bury, the premises were acquired by the Western Times sometime after 1788. Charles Dickens, a friend of the editor Thomas Latimer, is reputed to have stayed here in 1839.

143 Fore Street, for 60 years the home of the company. Originally built in 1714 for a wealthy cloth merchant, it has historical associations with famous personalities of the 19th century, including Charles Dickens.

1906 Wheatons was incorporated as a limited company.

1907 Sales for the trading year to 31 March were £21,236. The net profit was £210. The Managing Director's salary was £350 per annum.

1910–1914 Wheatons commenced educational publishing. The first title was *Wheatons' Observation Drawing Cards* – two sets at 2s 6d per packet. This was followed by *Wheatons' Brushwork Drawing Sheets* in a card folio at 15s per set.

Later publications included *Aid Copy Books, Essentials of Arithmetic & English, Combined Record Books* and other titles.

Wheatons engaged their first publishing representative to cover the Midlands.

1911 The company somewhat over-reached itself with the pace of the expansion into educational publishing and acquiring piecemeal properties at 143 Fore Street. Wheatons ran short of funds after having made losses for several years. Borrowing was at the limit of the facility with the company's bank and could not be extended.

A loan facility of £2,500 was arranged with a private money lender at an unknown level of interest. The loan was secured by £2,500 of the company's preference shares.

Having to borrow money in those days would have been very humiliating. To contribute to the company's funds, Chairman Alfred Wheaton let out his substantial residence in St Leonards, Exeter and moved into a modest property for a period of almost 5 years.

However, the new investment in publishing and resultant higher activity in the printing works began to pay off. The company returned to profitability and the loans were paid off by the beginning of World War I.

1914–1918 World War I commenced on 28 July 1914 and ended on 11 November 1918. There are no available records of company operations, if any, during this period.

1920 By 1920, Alfred's son Fred Wheaton, already in the business, considered that he had done enough good work for the company to be assigned some shares from his father. Alfred disagreed and an altercation ensued. Fred became so annoyed that he left the country and travelled to New Zealand with his family, including son John. There he joined educational publisher Whitcombe & Tombs.

The Letterpress Room in 1910. The large presses are Wharfedales stop cylinder machines all powered from an overhead drive shaft and belts from the gas engine. A row of Platen presses can be seen on the right of the picture. Note that all printers and apprentices are 'properly dressed' with starched collars and ties. By 1935 the company had upgraded the printed presses to electrically powered Miehles printing a sheet of up to 20 inches x 25 inches at 2,500 sheets per hour.

After a year Fred talked to his father again but with the same result. He vowed that he would not return unless formally invited back by his father. John, however, returned after 18 months to study engineering at Bristol University.

In 1922 Alfred announced he wished to retire. The Directors of the company, most of whom were family members, resolved that the most suitable candidate to take over the business was Fred. Fred accepted his father's invitation on agreeable terms and returned to become Chairman of the company.

Fred Wheaton, having acquired considerable experience in educational publishing with Whitcombe & Tombs in New Zealand, returned to become Chairman of the company and set about expanding the publishing list in junior and middle school books, reading schemes, atlases and other educational

A company staff outing in the 1920s, 73 staff present

materials. Fred embarked upon overseas educational book market sales development for three months of the year, with titles adapted for markets in South Africa, West Africa, Malaya, the Caribbean and the Pacific Islands. Later, sales agents were appointed in Nigeria, Jamaica and Malaya.

By 1921 a Mr Penuluma, previously of West Hill School, Dartford, Kent, already an author for Wheatons, was appointed Educational Advisor. He introduced potential authors. Mr Fortune Fowler, a geography teacher at a London County Council (LCC) school became an author. He in turn introduced Mr Crooks, a former president of the National Union of Teachers (NUT), who also became a regular author.

Mr Cyril Midgeley, previously of Mosley Grammar School, later joined Wheatons as Editor. His subject was geography and there followed a good stream of new material for publication.

The Educational Publishing Department became well established and built up a national reputation with a growing export market presence.

In 1921 the company employed some 75 staff. At a time when few Exeter companies were engaged in export, a third of the company's print production was shipped throughout much of the English-speaking world with the exception of the USA and India.

In the 1920s and the 1930s in particular, the company held an annual Waysgoose dinner for all staff. Waysgoose was a traditional entertainment function in the book printing and newspaper trades given by a Master Printer to his workforce each year. The function was held on St Bartholomew's Day and practised for hundreds of years. Waysgoose marked the end of summer and the start of the winter season, working by candlelight.

The practice was phased out at Wheatons after World War II when the

A staff motor charabanc outing to the countryside in 2 vehicles in 1925. Early charabancs were pulled by horses. Percy Poad, who joined the company in 1900, always made sure that he was one of the first on board to reach the back seats. Those who ended up at the front would have to endure the smell of horses passing wind or heavier ordinance!

The Letterpress Machine Room, 1927–1930. **Inset:** *An advertisement promoting the strength and virtues of the Wheaton cardboard box. Company Driver Bill Spiller is on the left.*

staff numbers increased significantly. There were also charabanc (open top coach) outings to the countryside and to other towns. Other long established printers in Exeter, including William Pollard & Co (founded 1822), and Besley & Copp (founded 1750) probably did the same.

1927 By this time the printing business, in factory premises at the rear of 143 Fore Street, had developed considerably. The company ran 11 printing machines and the larger presses were driven by belts to an overhead drive shaft powered from a large Crossley gas engine in the manner of a Lancashire cotton mill. A second engine drove a generator for the electric lighting in the factory. These engines had previously been used by the Western Times Company.

Letterpress printing, including typesetting, and hard-cased binding had been introduced by 1927. The educational book printing requirements of the publishing business were accommodated within the company. The company also became a major local manufacturer of cardboard boxes which were sold to the Exeter retail trade, fruit growers, etc *(see the illustration on page 18)*.

Before joining the business John Wheaton pursued his passion for motor cycles and launched AJW Motor Cycles *(see pages 36-47)* in 1926 in premises adjacent to the printing works. The machines became well respected in the market winning trials events and hill climbs as well as being touring bikes. The AJW business continued up to 1938 reaching production of up to 200 and finally a reputed 250 or more motor cycles per year before the war until sourcing of engine units became difficult and production was run down. In 1942 a fire destroyed the workshop, tools and patterns. After the war the business was sold and limited production was re-started.

1935 A successful Schools Contract Department was developed supplying school books, exercise books, library

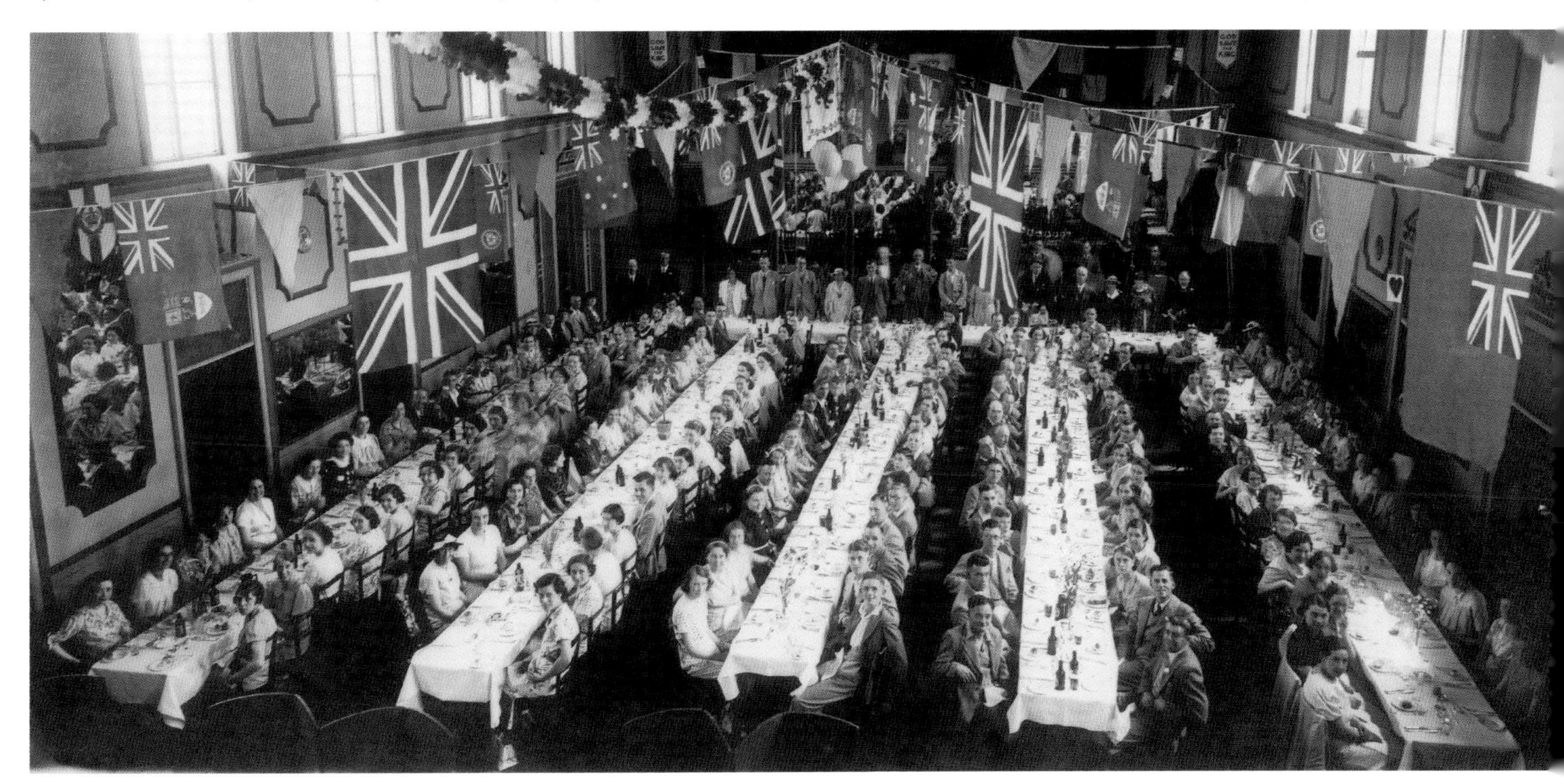

Wheaton's staff outing to Southsea in approximately 1935

books and stationery to county councils and libraries in the South West. It also supplied private schools and export customers. The company set up a Ruling Department to manufacture exercise books.

By 1935 the company employed 135 staff.

1938 John Wheaton joined the company and with his interest in plant and machinery considerably developed the printing works.

1940 World War II put a stop to everything. No further books were published and with few staff remaining the printing works were maintained with little activity during paper rationing. To make matters worse the company's two main lithographic printing machines were commandeered by the Americans and installed

Below: *Lackanooki, one of Wheatons' two inscribed Crabtree litho presses commandeered by the Americans to print invasion maps for D-Day covering the Normandy area. The machines were eventually located in a field near Cheltenham in 1946 and were restored to full working order by a Crabtree engineer. The company never received any compensation.*

Left: *A staff dinner at the Imperial Hotel ballroom in the 1930s*

at Cheltenham to print invasion maps for US troops after D-Day. Also, to avoid risk of enemy action, the Admiralty Chart Establishment at Cricklewood requisitioned two thirds of the bindery to print marine charts for three years whilst their new plant at Taunton was being built.

John Wheaton, as an engineer, was assigned to a senior management position at a large government armament training centre at Watford, working on aircraft instruments and aero-engine assembly for the rest of the war.

1942 On the night of 4 May, Wheatons' bookshop and offices, then at 231 and 232 High Street, along with much of the centre of Exeter around Bedford Street and Princesshay, was completely destroyed in a major air raid. This included the Accounts Department for the whole company. At the end of the war the bookshop was re-started in temporary basement premises in Queen Street.

The company's offices, including the Accounts Department, which had been bombed in High Street, were re-established at the 143 Fore Street premises.

An interior view of the bookshop in about 1935, prior to the bombing in 1942

Part of Wheaton's temporary underground retail premises in Gandy Street from 1942 – 1951 following the bombing of the High Street shop. The Gandy Street premises would certainly not have conformed to the Shops and Offices Act. There was no running water and there were no toilets but the 15 staff were allowed to use the conveniences at W H Smith Ltd and Surridge Dawson and Co. Water had to be brought into the shop for brewing tea.

These anti-aircraft cartridges were retrieved from the River Exe at Dawlish Warren during a diving trip by the author.

During the war there were approximately 19 German air raids on Exeter. A reported 265 people were killed and 788 injured, many seriously.

The Exe estuary would have been a key navigational aid for the Luftwaffa as it led to Exeter.

The first line of light defence against daytime low flying raiders was a battery of machine guns mounted on rafts in the river at the back of Dawlish Warren. Judging from shell cases of 1942 manufacture found littering the river bed at this point in 1980, these would have been Oerlikon or similar, 20 mm anti-aircraft guns.

The largest raid on the centre of Exeter occurred on the night of 4 May 1942 and was the most devastating. Twenty-eight bombers destroyed 400 shops, 150 offices, 50 warehouses and stores, and 36 clubs and pubs. Of the 20,000 houses in Exeter at the time, 1,500 were destroyed and 2,700 damaged.

Many of the air raids involved incendiary bombs. The Civil Defence ordered that all shop premises in the city centre should have fire wardens equipped to quell small roof fires quickly. Next door to Wheatons was Cummins Bookshop. The two shops set up a shared male-staff fire-watch rota whereby two men slept at the premises each night. All the Wheaton Directors of the bookshop business who were also fire wardens survived the war. There are no records of what happened on the night of 4 May 1942.

There were also loan wolf Messerschmitt ME109 strafing raids on Exeter streets. The ME109s came over from occupied northern France. After a brief raid they would retreat back across the Channel before the Polish Spitfire Squadron at Exeter Airport had time to scramble.

Later some office staff members regaled family and friends with stories of

The site of Wheaton's bookshop at 231 and 232 High Street after the Blitz

how, against advice, they had climbed out through the small door onto the roof parapet of 143 Fore Street to watch daytime bombing raids on Exeter!

Wheatons' Fore Street factory survived unscathed except for a fire which may have been started by an incendiary bomb and gutted the AJW motorcycle workshop. *(See page 47)*.

After the war, the planning and rebuilding of the High Street and Bedford Street areas, together with other parts of the city, took 20 years to complete.

1948 Recovery after the war was slow. There was difficulty in re-establishing the editorial team for the publishing business. To build up sales for the printing business, attention turned to the wider market of London book publishers. Mr P Dwerryhouse joined the company as Sales Director and successfully built up new business with London publishers and major companies in Devon and also acquired government printing contracts with His Majesty's Stationary Office (HMSO).

1950s The company directors and the management team in the early 1950s are shown on the right.

Chairman
Fred Wheaton

Joint Managing Directors
John Wheaton (Publishing) and **Roger Wheaton** (Works)

Retail Bookshop Directors
Harold Wheaton and **Eric Wheaton**

Sales Director
Philip Dwerryhouse

Finance Director and Company Secretary
W G Sharland (succeeded on his retirement in 1953 by **Leonard Rich**)

Accounts Department Manager
T Caddick

Stationery Contracts and Private Schools Manager
A W Guard

Exeter Contracts and Export Manager
Clifford Pullen

And foremen within the works:

Letterpress Department Foreman,
Norman Brown

Lithographic Department Foreman,
Gordon Tincombe

Composing Department Foreman,
George Lovering

Bindery Department Foreman,
Harold Gubb

Anstice Wheaton had already retired and **Roger Wheaton** was soon to do so.

The Wheaton Directors and the Managment Team between 1950 and 1960

Chairman Fred was a thrifty gentleman, a good businessman and salesman for the company. He was not practical, he could not change a light bulb nor knock in a nail. Yet he was a master of deck quoits on the passenger cargo ships steaming down to Africa when on his sales missions. The cargo ships carried just 12 passengers, the maximum permitted without a doctor on board. During the 9 months a year home in the 1950s he would play golf on Wednesday afternoons at Dawlish Warren Golf Club.

Mr John, his son, was highly practical and could make things and fix anything mechanical. Being opposites they made a successful pair for a publishing and printing business.

Left to right: *Fred Wheaton, Roger Wheaton, P A Dwerryhouse (Sales Director, Printing Department). W G Sharland (Company Secretary), A W Gard (Manager schools contacts), John Wheaton, Alf Cann (Lithographic machine minder).*

This management team built the company back up after World War II. Many staff, particularly in the factory departments, would have taken a year or more to adjust back to civilian life and routine working conditions after serving in the war.

Work-day etiquette in 1950 was still formal. Management wore suits in winter. Overseers wore white or brown overall coats. Shirt sleeves were acceptable in summer but always with a tie. Directors were addressed as Mr John, Mr Roger, etc. and managers and overseers as Mr Brown, Mr Gubb, etc.

Left to right: *(Front row) John Wheaton, Eric Wheaton, Fred Wheaton, W G Sharland (Company Secretary) Clifford Pullen (in charge of Exeter contract and export), A W Gard (in charge of Devon contract and Private Schools), Harold Wheaton. (Back row) T Caddick (Accounts Department.) and J E Thomson (Editor).*

Standards became more relaxed, American style, in the 1960s and at Marsh Barton, but ties remained. Production staff wore aprons in Comps (the Composition Department) and the bindery, bib and brace or overalls in the machine rooms.

Wheatons' Services to Commerce and Education was conducted at Fore Street under the management of Mr A W Guard. The department operated from a three-storey warehouse building in Friernhay Street, adjacent to the printing factory and was a separate enterprise from the bookshop.

The 137-page 1950s Commerce and Education catalogue covered all office supplies including desks and chairs, typewriters, filing cabinets, filing systems, account books, pencils, rulers and sundries, blotters and stationery. The department developed into school supplies and exercise books and also held, for some years, the contract to supply Devon County Libraries.

Wheatons' large blue delivery van was known by most private and independent schools in Devon and the wider area and was always driven by long-standing employee Bill Spiller.

On Mr Guard's retirement, Mr Andrews became the manager. New premises were built for the department in the 1960s in Christow Road, Marsh Barton. The business later moved again to within the new factory building until it was sold to Oyez Stationers in 1986.

From the 1950s to the 1980s, Wheatons were members of the British Federation of Master Printers – South Western Alliance. The local branch was the Exeter and District Master Printers Association who met regularly at The Devon and Exeter Institution, 7 Cathedral Yard. The meetings were held in the library amongst the musty aroma of old leather bound books – the work of previous printers 150 years before.

The Association secretaries, including Anthony Wheaton, had the job of whipping in busy members to attend the meetings but when it came to wage negotiation time with the unions they would all be there, including those from Plymouth and Barnstaple.

1953 Mr Leonard Rich – Company Finance Director was later to become Managing Director. John Wheaton was to become Chairman of the company.

Winter heating was always a problem in the Fore Street factory and getting through to March without trouble was a challenge for management. 1953 was a particularly cold winter.

The heating system in the factory had no radiators but overhead cast iron piping of about 3 inches diameter – most of the heat therefore rose into the apex of the roof. In the printing machine room area there was some additional warming from the large electric motors and male machine minders all wore boiler suits so they kept reasonably warm.

In the bindery it was a different matter. On one occasion a deputation of bindery girls were sent up by the Foreman to the Work Director's office to complain that it was just over 50° F in the bindery and too cold for handwork jobs. He had to tell them that the boiler had been running on maximum since 5 a.m. but he would see if anything further could be done.

At the next board meeting it was approved that Exeter's main heating contractor Garton & King would be instructed to add two more cast iron sections to the 1930s boiler to increase capacity. They had noted that the Factory Act required a minimum maintained temperature for workers of 60° F.

143 Fore Street was four storeys high and built on the steep hill. On the lower side was an alleyway, a side entrance to

the printing works. There was no support from neighbouring buildings for the high side wall, that had been built in 1714. One night an alarming half-inch wide crack appeared on the inside wall which could be followed up the staircase through two floors from the offices to the Editorial and Artist's Department.

The company architect, Mr Challice, would have been called. As there was no bulge apparent on the outside brickwork, it was resolved that strips of brown paper tape would be applied every 2 feet, dated and signed, for frequent monitoring. By 1973 the paper had not split and the wall had therefore not moved again.

1959 After National Service in the army and having completed a two-year executive training course at the London School of Printing and Graphic Arts (LSPGA), John's son, Anthony Wheaton, joined the business as assistant to Roger Wheaton, Works Director, at a salary of £500.

An important annual contract at this time was the Western National Omnibus Company (WNOC) bus timetables. The timetables covered all routes in Devon and the wider area. The work had to be completed before the publication of new or revised routes and timings and had to be in the possession of all bus conductors before they could operate.

The timetable pages were rolled over year on year and updated from standing type metal pages in small 8 pt type. The work went on for weeks in the Composing Room with Wheaton's longest serving staff member, Percy Poad, acting as a runner at least twice a day between the company and WNOC's office in Queen Street. He would convey new copy, first proofs, revised proofs and signed off proofs for the period of the contract. He lived on the job and walked everywhere.

Percy Poad of Sydney Road joined the company at the age of 14 in 1900. His starting salary was £5.4s.0d per annum. He became Wheatons' first outdoor stationery supplies salesman working out of the Queen Street–High Street bookshop. When he eventually retired he had served 65 years of unbroken service.

A national UK printing strike took place at about this time.

Wheatons' main paper supplier was Reed and Smith at Silverton Mill just north of Exeter. Mill representative Mr Yeo visited Roger Wheaton and later Anthony Wheaton at 2 p.m. on Fridays to take the next orders.

The Mill formulated a bespoke bulky cartridge paper for educational book printing. Paper was delivered to

Waste not, want not

David Lee joined the company aged 15, in 1957, to work in the Work Study office. During the National Printing Strike in about 1958, there was little to do in the printing company. David was sent up to the High Street shop by Roger Wheaton, Works Director, to do something useful. He was to learn about the value of thrift.

David's first daily task became unpacking parcels of incoming stock but, explained Mr Fred Wheaton (Chairman), he was to 'undo all the knots in the string carefully and wind it up for reuse when we send out parcels to customers. Look after the pennies and the pounds will look after themselves'.

David retired in 2006 after 49 years of continuous service. In later years his main role in the company was invoicing which involved picking up all the extras which could justifiably be charged to customers. His early training had served him well.

The print room in the 1960s

The busy bindery department at Fore Street in 1965

the Bartholomew Street loading dock in individually wrapped reams of 500 plus sheets. There were no fork lift trucks at the time. Reams were hand carried to pallet trucks by warehouse man Bob Sharp.

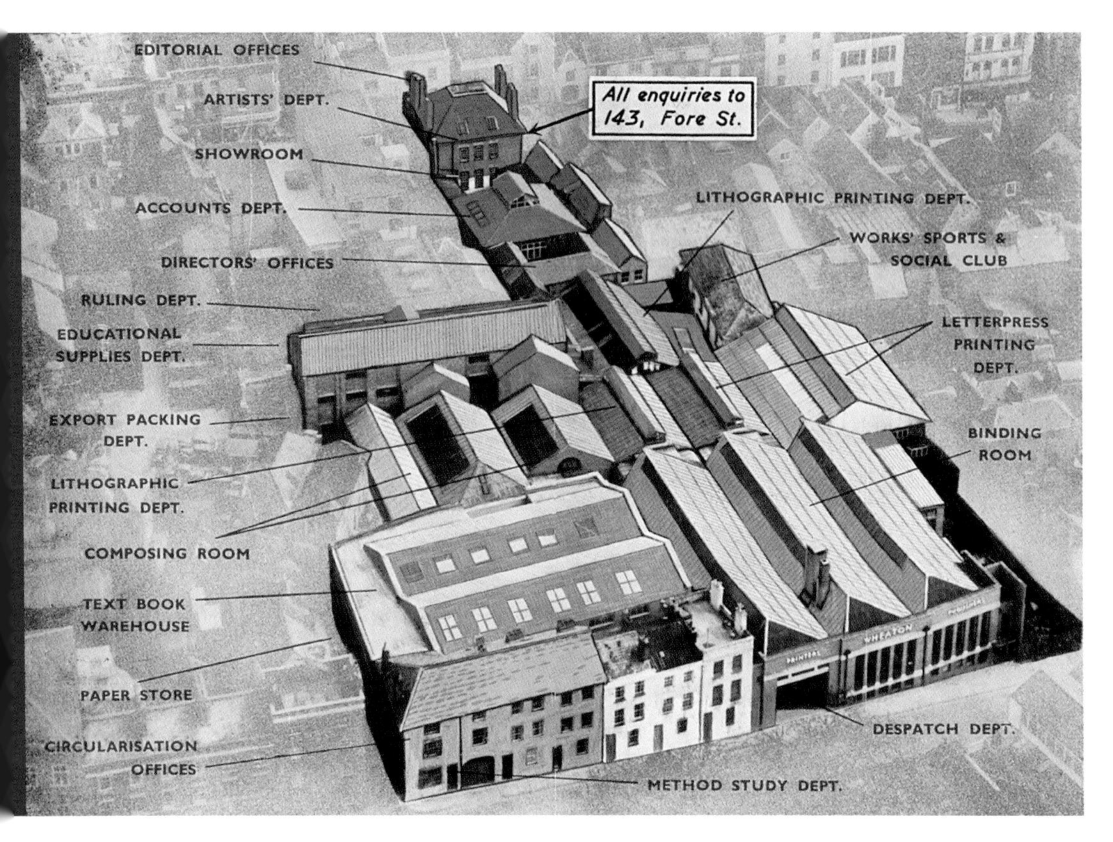

A 1960s aerial view of the Fore Street offices and factory departments. The last building to be completed in 1956 was to accommodate the textbook warehouse and paper store. The premises extended from Fore Street hill through to Bartholomew Street. Apart from 143 Fore Street, the rest of the site was developed for housing after the company moved to Marsh Barton.

1964 In March Anthony Wheaton was appointed Works Manager on the retirement of Roger Wheaton. He later became Works Director. Frank Wright was appointed Assistant Works Manager.

1965 By now, the Fore Street factory and offices of some 65,000 square feet in the centre of Exeter was becoming restricting for the business. The company was beginning to receive frequent complaints from nearby residents of machine noise on overtime, and traffic congestion on the narrow street at the rear of the factory. To provide for the future, a 6 acre greenfield development site was acquired at Marsh Barton Trading Estate.

In October 1960 Exeter and mid-Devon had had in excess of 440 mm of rain in ten days. On 27th October 'Black Thursday' the River Exe burst its banks and flooded much of the Exwick and St Thomas area of Exeter to a depth of 5 to 7 feet.

The choice of low-lying Marsh Barton for the new factory site was therefore not straightforward. An alternative was the Sowton Trading Estate on the east side of Exeter but this was still at the planning stage and on sloping land best suited to smaller developments.

The Marsh Barton Estate development was well ahead with road layouts and services already installed. To reduce risk of future flooding, the road levels were already raised by one metre *(see page 55)*. The land was flat and more suitable for a large factory floor area without ramps. Added to which, most of Wheatons' staff lived on the west side of Exeter.

The Marsh Barton site was chosen after the 1962 Exeter flood relief channels were built with £8 million of government aid. Also, the banks of the Alphin Brook, which had flooded parts of Marsh Barton in the past, were raised.

However, it was deemed prudent to also raise the whole of the factory area by one metre to road level and to install sumps in the floor to aid pumping out any future floodwater which may enter the building.

The new bindery was built first. Printing continued at Fore Street for several more years with printed sheets transported on pallets by lorry twice daily to Marsh Barton.

At this time the company had some 250 employees.

Meanwhile, the bookshop had now moved from Queen Street back to the High Street, close to the Guildhall, and continued trading there until 1967 when the premises were sold.

Creating an image

In 1965 Dennis Wrigley was appointed as the company's design consultant to formulate a coordinated style and layout policy for Wheatons' publications and to give the range of stationery a new look.

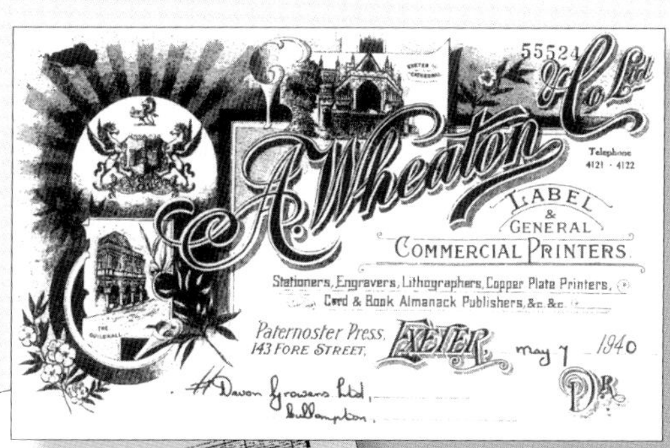

The elaborately engraved headings of the company's invoice sets reproduced here were still in use until after 1945. This heading demonstrated the skill of the company's art designers and engravers from Victorian times. Such engraved headings were a popular style for stationery amongst Exeter companies at the time.

A modern style for the time was introduced from about 1966 incorporating logos from printing and publishing, stationery supplies and a general letterhead depicting a drawing of 143 Fore Street. This illustration was created by Geoffrey Fraser (son of Eric Fraser, illustrator to the Radio Times).

WHEATON *of* EXETER

This logo was used by the Educational Publishing Department in the late 1950s.

A letterhead used by the publishing department in 1964

A 'Zinco' of 143 Fore Street

Before lithography a 'wood block' or a 'Zinco' was the only way printers could transfer a drawing or piece of artwork to paper. To produce half-tone or line blocks 'photocopying' copy is done by fixing the original in front of the camera. Copy can only be enlarged or reduced in proportion by the camera and, therefore, all originals must reduce or enlarge by a previously decided proportion before the copy goes to camera.

When a sensitised film or plate is exposed to light and then developed, the areas affected by light appear dense on the negative and the areas not affected by light remain transparent.

The developed film or plate is a negative or, in other words, the complete opposite of the original.

In block making the negative has to be printed on to a metal plate to form a printing surface, which in letterpress printing, has to be the reverse of that required when finally printed on a paper. A prism placed in front of the camera produces the negative in which the image appears the same way round as the original. This provides the required effect for relief printing.

The negative is now ready for use and is printed down on to a smooth metal surface, which normally is made of zinc, hence the trade name Zinco. The area is coated in light-sensitive material which is then exposed to light through the negative. The light hardens the light-sensitive material and when developed the unhardened material washes away. The light-hardened image is then inked up and dusted with an acid-resisting powder known as dragon's blood. The zinc is then etched and then the acid bites into the metal which has not been protected by the acid resisting-material, you thus obtain a printing surface in relief which is known as a Zinco.

1. The original drawing or artwork

2. The image is transfered to a zinc plate via photography and then acid etched. The 'Zinco' is then mounted on a wooden block.

3. The 'Zinco' is then inked when on the press and transfered via the printing press to the paper.

The bookshop finally moved to 143 Fore Street before closing in about 1971 after 133 years of trading.

The bookshop and stationery side of the business were managed over the years by Fred's brothers, Anstice and Harold, and later by Harold's son, Eric. By 1968 all had retired from the business. The bookshops and the stationery businesses always returned a modest profit but they were not a significant enough part of the business to interest Pergamon Press for the future.

At the 1965 Exeter School of Printing annual ceremony, nine of the company's apprentices were nominated in the City & Guilds categories of letterpress printing, composing, industry awards, book binding, office administration, estimating and typographical design. Their awards were rated best craft and credit. One further apprentice received a certificate for typographical design in the British Printing Industries Federation (BPIF) Design for Printing competition.

The printing industry experienced a downturn leading to much increased trade competition in the book production sector. A BPIF report was commissioned in 1965 to forecast the way the industry was likely to develop. The author of the report, Mr Brec, an economist, concluded with the view that large and small commercial printing firms would survive but that medium size printers, including book printers, of 100–150 staff would probably be squeezed out or merged.

1966 The acquisition of book printer D R Hillman of Frome, Somerset was Wheatons first venture into serious colour printing.

Hillmans produced colour books and commercial packaging print to a quality standard to which Wheatons could not yet aspire. Initially, geography books and atlases published by Wheatons and Pergamon Press were sent to Hillmans to print on their large format Sovereign SP 5-colour press.

Later, Hillmans main printing plant including the Sovereign were moved to Exeter and installed at Fore Street, after the bindery had moved to Marsh Barton. A number of key production staff moved to Exeter from Frome.

Hillmans were already working with several London-based publishers of colour illustrated children's books. Wheatons planned to build on this base to enter the children's book market.

Unfortunately, the Sovereign press could not be kept sufficiently occupied

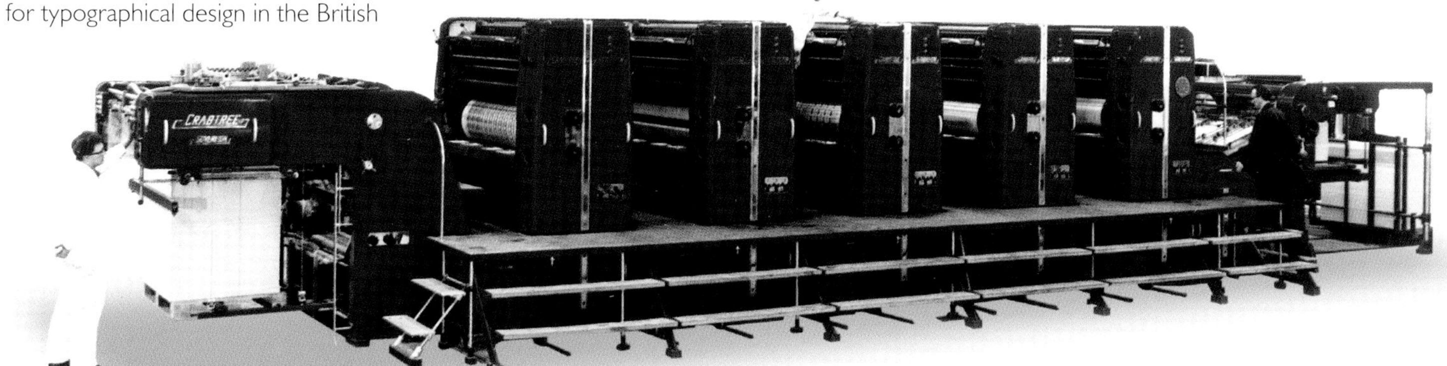

The Crabtree 5-colour Sovereign printing press installed at Fore Street. The machine was transfered from Hillmans, Frome in 1967.

A selection of early company catalogues

for commercial viability and was sold to a greetings card printer. Colour book work continued on two of Hillmans, Mann 2-colour presses.

An employee from Hillmans, Barry Burt, became a long serving staff member and went on to become an Exeter City Labour Councillor (St Thomas' Ward).

From the mid-1960s, whilst at Fore Street, the company published their own house magazine – *Number 143*. The magazine contained an editorial from the company including news and announcements, and reports and information from the thriving Sports & Social Club.

Over the 1960s and 1970s the company encouraged apprenticeships and usually took up the full quota set between the Master Printers Association (later BPIF) and the Printing & Kindred Trades Federation of the unions.

Indentured apprentices underwent craft training over a period of 2 to 5 years during which time they could not leave the company. Apprentices attended the Exeter College of Printing in the Mint conveniently close to the Fore Street factory. They attended 'day release' courses locally and 'block release' courses at Bristol College of Printing to attain NVQ qualifications for the trade in composing, print and book binding.

Qualified as journeymen, the ex-apprentices played an important part in the company becoming key craftsmen and supervisors, and some became managers. On qualifying, ex-apprentices were free to leave the company and pursue careers with other printers but many remained with the company.

From the early 1960s publishing educational books for overseas markets became progressively more difficult. Countries were gaining independence from the Commonwealth and changing their names and boundaries. It became challenging to keep atlases up to date on a commercially viable basis. New countries were no longer prepared to accept adapted school books by English authors. It was necessary to use local school teacher authors and preferably to publish the books in conjunction with a local publishing house as well.

Wheatons began to lose out in the export market to developing local publishers and to much larger British educational publishers. These were able to heavily invest in building up reputations for books published specifically for overseas English-speaking countries with local involvement rather than using adapted material.

The publishing department was by now not providing the volume of printing enjoyed in earlier years so the company became more dependent on outside publishers' work. Added to this, the printing works was much in need of reinvestment to remain competitive as metal type letterpress printing declined in favour of film process lithography.

The printing business always worked on a 10% profit mark up on costs of production for work undertaken for other company departments. These included Educational Publishing (books), School Stationery (exercise books and ruled paper) and the Retail Shop (personal stationery orders).

1966–7 After opening a new book production account with fast expanding scientific and academic publisher Pergamon Press in Oxford, it became apparent that closer co-operation could be beneficial. Pergamon was interested in moving into educational publishing, Wheatons had the printing expertise to manufacture Pergamon's books and with new investment, their journals as well. Robert Maxwell made an offer for the company.

The offer had to be given careful consideration. The directors debated the following main matters:

- The publishing business had for some time found its overseas markets becoming increasingly difficult and could see no early prospect for improvement
- The printing factory was very dependent on the Publishing Department for its own prosperity, with 50% of its profitable bookwork coming from this source
- The printing factory was very much geared to book production – a market well catered for at the time by other well-known large general book printers. To increase work from this market would involve giving lengthy credit to publishers and so tying up working capital
- The price offered for Wheatons' shares was such that the shareholders could reinvest the proceeds at a much higher return on capital than they were currently receiving. It had been the policy of the company directors to plough back a considerable proportion of the annual profits for future development but this policy reduced the level of distribution to the shareholders
- Much of the printing and binding plant was becoming due for replacement but the company would not be able to raise sufficient capital without onerous new borrowing commitments
- Some directors had retired and others were soon to do so. In 1966 widows of the family directors who had outlived their husbands were not exempt from paying death duties on their husbands' estates. It was probable that widows would be forced to sell inherited shares to pay the duty. (The law has now changed on this matter.)

Pergamon's offer to acquire the business had come at a convenient time and it was agreed to formally respond to the offer.

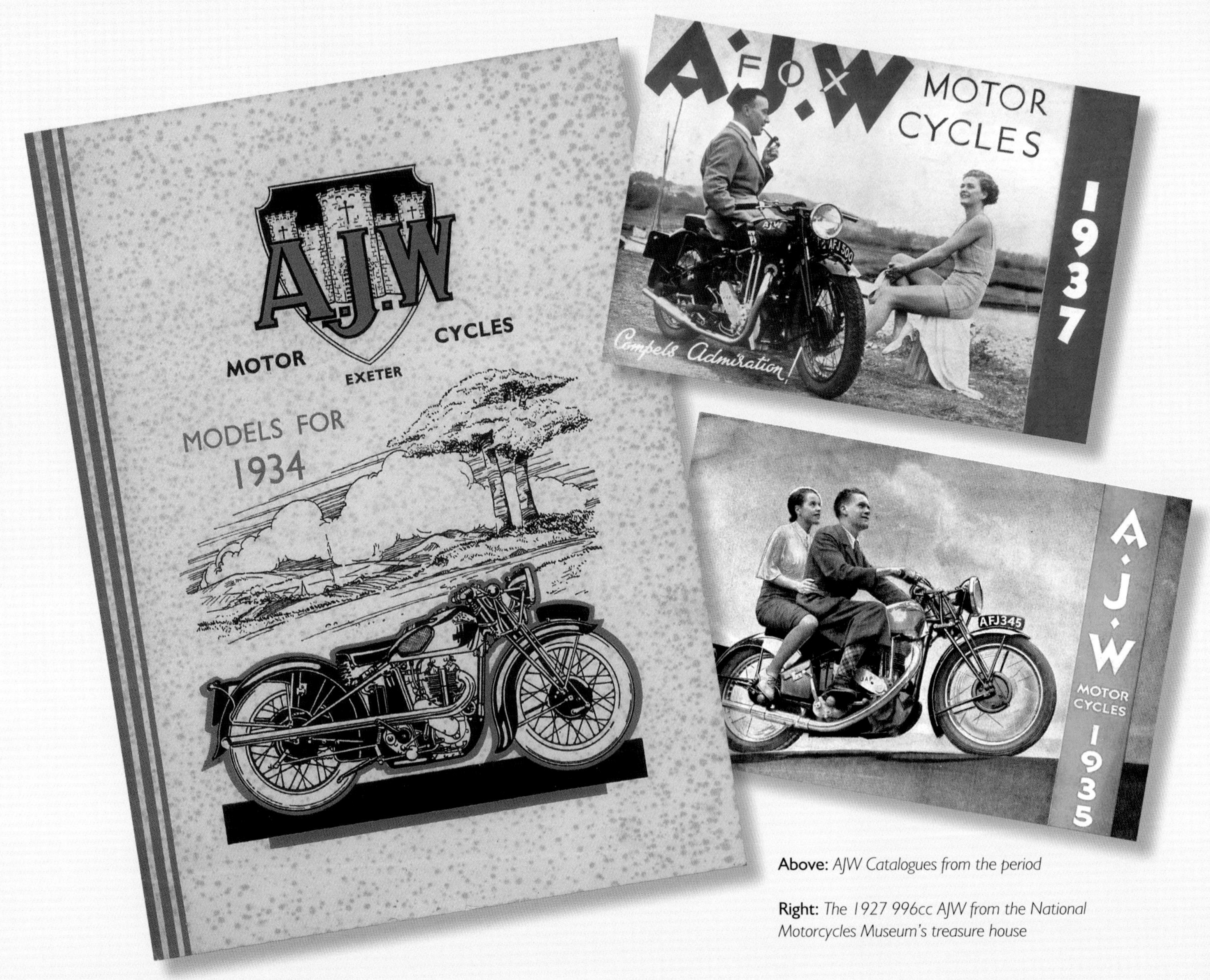

Above: *AJW Catalogues from the period*

Right: *The 1927 996cc AJW from the National Motorcycles Museum's treasure house*

AJW Motorcycles

John Wheaton's keen interest in motorcycles started when he was still a schoolboy, having been allowed to ride his father's motorcycle at about the age of 16. Like train spotters, he and his friends could tell any make of machine by its exhaust note and could recite its specification. One day he vowed to build his own 'ideal' machine.

John attended engineering courses and worked with a motorcycle manufacturer in Birmingham. His family moved to New Zealand for a few years where his father Fred joined educational publishers Whitcombe & Tombs.

John then joined an engineering business in New Zealand and during this time rode around the whole of the South Island on very rudimentary roads, sometimes fording rivers. On his return to England he attended Bristol University and gained a diploma in engineering.

1920s Fred Wheaton returned from New Zealand to become Chairman of Wheatons. John was allowed to pursue his interest in motorcycles, experimenting with design ideas of his own in the printing company's Engineering Maintenance Department.

By 1926 he knew exactly what he wanted to do. Inspired by motorcycle company Brough of Nottingham (of Lawrence of Arabia fame), he designed his own rather similar twin-cylinder machine but using different components and a welded duplex frame design. The Brough Superior V twin machine was the established top-end market leader and the benchmark for AJW on price.

At this stage John only intended to build a machine for his own use. The first AJW was built in spare time in a small workshop in Exeter with the help of a friend. The AJW was a low profile layout just 30 inches high. After extensive research the choice of engine was a British Anzani Vulpine V twin overhead valve of 996 cc also known as a Summit engine, but they were in fact the same unit. John was particularly impressed with the valve operating mechanism of the Vulpine. As engines became more powerful, valve spring breakages had begun to plague the sporting and road-going machines alike. On side-valve engines a broken spring meant that the valve dropped back into its seat without damage. However on overhead valve layouts, the valve stems protruded vertically from the cylinder head and were subject to heat, and the springs could become brittle. On a spring failure, the valve would be free to drop into the combustion chamber and smash the piston.

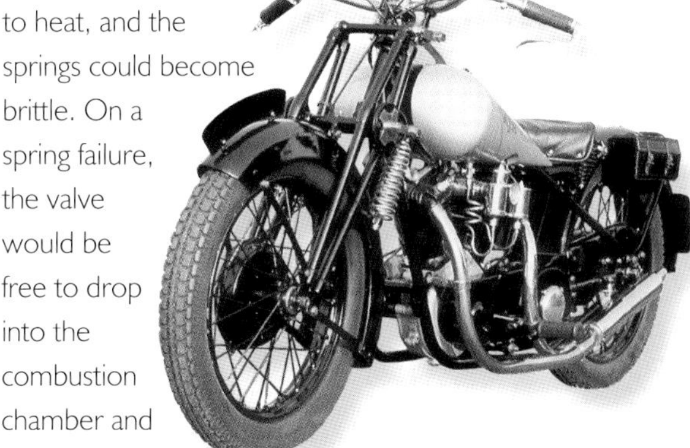

The Vulpine design avoided this danger by inclining the inlet and exhaust valves at 45% to the cylinder head and extending well into the cool airstream. This approach ensured that the springs were cooled and proved to be a reliable solution.

Finally the great day came for the first road test. The bike seemed to be an absolute winner, acceleration was colossal, steering really good and everything worked just as it should. The few improvements necessary were soon made.

The bike was driven for several thousand miles all over the country. Then, with side car added, John drove it to Switzerland and back. Within a year the machine had covered a distance of some 10,000 miles and was well proven.

At a time when motorcycles generally had single cylinder side-valve engines of about 500 or 600 cc, the choice of the Vulpine twin-cylinder engine put the AJW almost in a class of its own. The Vulpine with Binks 3-jet carburettor matched up to a Jardin 4-speed gear box, another newcomer to the motor cycle world, proved an ideal combination.

With confidence high, John, who also became known in motorcycling circles as Jack, entered his AJW for a high speed trial run held at Brooklands race track. The event attracted admirers and much interest from the motoring press. A reporter from *Classic Motorcycle* magazine took pictures and an extensive editorial was published in the next issue. In the days after publication John received a sheaf of letters from motorcyclists asking for particulars.

With start-up capital provided by his father, John started a small business to manufacture the model in late 1926. The AJW Motor Company was launched from a small warehouse adjacent to the Fore Street printing works in Friernhay Street and initially employed the services of Sidney Hutt, son of Wheatons' engineer. The first firm order came from a Welsh enthusiast who was lent the prototype for six months whilst the first 'production model' was built and tested.

Orders started to come in and production commenced in a small way using the Vulpine engine. Later, other models with the same frame design with modifications were added, using JAP engines of 840 cc overhead valve single cylinder. In 1927, 20 Vulpine-engined machines were built. Each motorcycle was hand built and tailored to customers' requirements – including such optional extras as electric lights.

1928 The AJW company was becoming established and appointed agents in Vienna, Budapest (whose first order was for five machines), Switzerland and Johannesburg.

A radical new design of machine was built to attempt the motorcycle world speed record. Named the Super 4 it was based on a supercharged Coventry Climax 4-cylinder water-cooled car engine of 985 cc. An Anzani engine was also installed

A·J·W· MOTOR COMPANY, LTD.
FRIERNHAY STREET, EXETER, ENG.
MANUFACTURERS OF A.J.W. MOTOR CYCLES

Your Ref.............
Our Ref.............
Date.............

The letterhead for the A. J. W Motor Company Ltd

Left: *The first of the 'Kneelers'. The 'Kneelers' concept using a low-level layout with a 985cc 4-cylinder Anzani car engine. This machine was designed for an attempt to break the motorcycle speed record in 1929. Trial development runs of the prototype took place at first light on Saturday mornings on the only straight road sections near Exeter. These were the Rockbeare Straight on the A30 and the Pinhoe to Silverton Beare Straight on the B3181. The later was favoured with fewer inhabitants living nearby.*

There were no tailored motoring leathers available at the time. Rider George Tucker was bound up with insulating tape on arms and legs to prevent clothes flapping and to improve aerodynamics. Speeds of over 100 mph were recorded but the unstable geometry of the steering design proved a difficult problem and ultimately resulted in the attempt being abandoned. The final tests took place at the Brooklands race track and in France.

at some point. Exhibited on the AJW stand at the1928 London Olympia Motorcycle Show, security men had to be hired to hold back the crowd such was the interest.

The following year the AJW Super 4 was taken to Brooklands and then to Arpagon in France for a world speed record attempt, driven by Bristol road racer George Tucker. Unfortunately, at high speed the machine proved to be unstable and the attempt was abandoned. The front suspension and steering system were most unconventional and design problems were never satisfactorily rectified. The Super 4 never went into production.

Right: *The Super 4 drew 1928 Olympia crowds to the AJW stand, but it was no record breaker.*

Through the night. John Wheaton navigating a forest section on a long distance trial with sidecar in about 1927.

There was no better test bed for man and machine than the arduous motorcycle trials of the late 1920s and 1930s. AJW machines competed regularly in the main events staged by the Motorcycling Club of Great Britain.

The London to Lands End 1927 sidecar event was won by John Wheaton and Fred Knill on an AJW Vulpine machine. They had made the fastest climb on a timed section of the notorious Beggars Roost Hill near Lynmouth, north Devon to win gold medal. John won gold and silver medals in the 1927 International 6-Day Trial. There were also first class awards for the 1926 Yeovil to Land's End trial among many others.

The gruelling test for dependability was the cross country competition trials over rough tracks, with steep rock strewn gullies and mud, water and more mud. All these conditions led to robust dependability of design and fully tested components.

AJWs were exhibited annually at Olympia, London and created considerable interest among enthusiasts. With the light blue fuel tank, twin port straight exhausts and V twin engine, the AJW was an attractive well balanced design. Machines were later sold in France, Australia, Canada and the USA.

1927 The price for an AJW with Vulpine engine capable of 100 mph was £115 –£145. A small car could be bought at the time for £110. AJW was therefore operating at the top end of the market and motorcyclist customers had to be very keen indeed to spend that kind of money. A pattern was emerging – the AJW was an exclusive motorcycle selling to wealthy buyers – but it was also a limited market.

Wheatons' first motocycle – registered as a AJW in April 1926

1927 SUCCESSES.

London—Exeter	1 A.J.W. entered	1 Gold
London—Lands End	3 " "	2 Golds 1 retired broken Side-Car spindle.
		1 Silver Cup (highest award).
London—Holyhead	1 " "	do. do.
Brighton—Beer	1 " "	do. do.
London—Coventry	1	do. do.
Sunbeam 200	1 " "	1 Gold
International 6 days	2 " "	1 Silver
West of England 1 day trial	1 A.J.W. Sidecar entered	Secured Silver Cup for best performance of Sidecar over 600 c.c.

1928.

A. J.W. MOTOR COMPANY,

Friernhay Street, EXETER.

Telephone : Exeter

A. WHEATON & CO., LTD., EXETER.

A.J.W. 9.96 Standard.

Saddle Height, 24½ in. Wheel Base, 58 in. Ground Clearance, 4½ in.

Price £115 : 0 : 0

SPECIFICATION.

ENGINE. British Vulpine, 996 c.c. V Twin, having a Bore of 78 m/m., Stroke 104. Cylinders, set at an angle of 57° are made from special close grain cast iron, the bores being ground and lapped to ensure great accuracy. The Cylinder heads are of a spherical design, machined inside all over to fine limits; inlet and exhaust ports are of large diameter, giving a very free passage for gas.

The Crankshaft is of built-up pattern having counter weighted internal flywheels specially balanced. A double ball bearing is fitted to the crankshaft on the driving side and a large roller bearing on the timing side, and the extreme end of the shaft is supported by a ball-bearing fitted in the cover of the timing case.

The camshaft is of strong design, the cams which operate the tappet rods being detachable; the rocker levers are fitted with rollers of ample size, which are hardened and mounted on floating bushes.

Pistons are constructed of hard wearing die-cast aluminium alloy, with dome shaped tops, each being fitted with three piston rings, the lower one acting as an oil scraper.

Gudgeon pins are hollow and of large diameter, fully floating in both piston and connecting rod, brass caps being fitted to both ends to prevent scoring the cylinder. The connecting rods, which are stamped from high tensile steel, are H section, and fitted with a roller big end bearing.

Two valves are fitted to each cylinder at an angle of 45°. They are of large diameter, and made from steel specially suitable for the purpose. These valves are operated by overhead rockers encased in neat oil retaining and dustproof aluminium cases, fitted to the tops of the cylinder heads.

MAGNETO. M.L., mounted on a platform on the side of the timing case, driven by silent bevel gears.

CARBURETTOR. Binks 2 Jet Model, fitted with twist grip throttle control. (The famous 3 Jet mouse trap can be fitted as an extra if required.)

TRANSMISSION is by Coventry ⅝ × ⅜ chain to Jardine four-speed gear-box, and thence by another Coventry chain of the same size to the Enfield cush hub situated in the rear wheel.

The Jardine gear-box is a particularly fine piece of work, the 4 speeds being obtained with the same number of gear wheels as in the usual 3 speed.

The outside casting has a remarkably smooth contour, free from dirt accumulating corners, in the form of the maker's name, etc.

All gears are constantly in mesh, being provided with dogs for gear changing, so that the gear teeth are not liable to be chipped or damaged.

The patented gear control consists of a long lever fitted to the gear box itself. Thus, when once adjusted by the makers, the gear cannot possibly get out of adjustment.

A very large clutch, operated by a Bowden lever on the left handlebar, is fitted to these boxes, giving a beautifully sweet action.

FRAME. Specially low built duplex cradle type, made entirely in one piece. The Duplex Triangular construction gives immense rigidity at all speeds, and whip, which is almost bound to occur in the single type of frame, is entirely eliminated. In addition to giving a remarkably low riding position, the frame protects the engine from possible damage, due to large rocks or projections in the road, often to be met with in competition work.

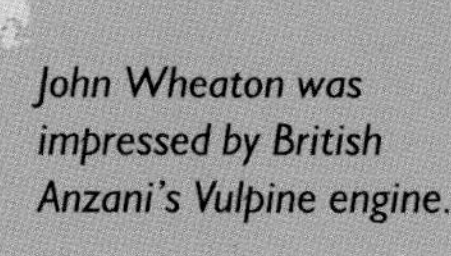

John Wheaton was impressed by British Anzani's Vulpine engine.

WHEELS. These are built up with Dunlop Rims, 9 gauge spokes and Enfield 8" hub brakes front and rear. The back wheel is fitted with the famous Enfield cush drive.

Both wheels are quickly detachable, the removal of the front wheel being effected merely by loosening the axle nuts and removing a small pin holding the brake connection. The wheel is then free to fall out.

Removal of the rear wheel is almost as simple. First loosen the axle nuts, thus rendering the chain adjusters removable without the use of tools, owing to specially slotted lugs. Now slacken the wing nut which releases the brake rod, and the wheel may be kicked forward until it drops out.

TYRES are Dunlop Cords, either wired-on type (26 × 3.25) fitted on Well Base Rims, or 26 × 3 (700 × 80) beaded edge type.

FORKS. Druid A.R.T. triangulated girder type, tremendously strong and rigid, fitted with large adjustable shock absorbers; or the "Maclean,"—the low unsprung weight and trailing link action of which eliminates wheel bounce and speed wobble.

TANK. Saddle type, of exceptionally handsome design, having a bulbous nose. These tanks are fitted with quick action filler caps.

The oil tank is connected to that containing petrol in such a way that they cannot possibly leak one into the other. The oil tank being actually obscured by the other, the whole retains the neat appearance of a single tank.

This tank has a capacity of—Petrol, 2½ gallons; Oil, 3 pints.

BRAKES. Great care has been given to Brake design. A toe pedal on the left side of the machine applies both front and rear brakes, which are inter-connected. A massive Bowden lever on the right handle-bar also applies both brakes, and this lever is fitted with a ratchet whereby the machine may be left on a hill with both wheels locked.

Independent operation of the front brake is obtained by an inverted lever on the left handlebar.

MUDGUARDS are particularly effective, being of 7" section, beautifully shaped and finished. These are made of very heavy gauge metal, which will last the life time of the machine.

SADDLE. The world-famous "Leckie" Super Sports with shock absorbers, about which no more need be said.

SILENCER. Large diameter plated Exhaust Pipes with pleasing curves, lead into an expansion chamber of special design, which effectively reduces noise with an almost total absence of back pressure.

LUBRICATION is by mechanical pump. A Best and Lloyd hand pump is also fitted, and a two-way tap is arranged so that oil may either be directed to chains or to the rocker boxes.

Lubrication of the cycle parts is by Tecalemit grease gun system.

HANDLEBARS are made from high quality steel, and are adjustable to suit all riding positions.

CHAIN CASES are quickly detachable, and made from aluminium, and are highly polished.

TOOL BAG. One large tool bag is fitted under the saddle in a position where it is subject to very little road vibration—a comprehensive tool kit being provided as standard equipment with each machine.

STANDS are fitted for both front and rear wheels. The rear stand (of spring-up type) fitted below the gear-box. In addition to these, there is an exceedingly neat prop stand.

A.J.W. 8.30 Standard.

Price £125 : 0 : 0

Or fitted with 8 h.p. Sports J.A.P. Engine, at £115 : 0 : 0

This model, with the exception of the Engine and Exhaust System, is identical to the 9.96 Standard fully described above.

A.J.W. "Double-Port" Special.

Price: Fully Equipped, £170 : 0 : 0

Less Equipment, £155 : 0 : 0

A.J.W. 8.45 Special.

Price: Fully Equipped, £170 : 0 : 0

Less Equipment, £155 : 0 : 0

SPECIAL PROSPECTUS ON APPLICATION.

73

Photo: The Vintage Motor Cycle Club Archives

1930s In October 1929 the US Wall Street Stock Market Crash occurred leading to the 'Great Depression' of 1931 and 1932 in the UK.

By 1931, sourcing of parts was becoming difficult. The price for the Vulpine engined machine had reached £170, the same price as George Brough's JAP powered SS100. Sales were falling off and production of this model ceased later in the year when Anzani discontinued manufacture of this engine.

To address a wider market the AJW company developed a range of lower powered single cylinder machines. The mid-field market of 350 cc and 500 cc machines was well catered for by competitors – Rudge, HRD, Gridley Peerless, Cotton, etc. Consequently AJW set out to build lightweight 2 strokes from 150 cc to 350 cc where there was less competition. Five Villiers-powered models using Albion 3-speed gearboxes were launched these being Black Fox 122 cc and 196 cc and Silver Fox of 247 cc and 343 cc and another. The 2 strokes sold well but at a lower price range. With limited manufacturing capacity, John soon realised that he needed higher value products to keep AJW profitable.

1931 A new model was designed to compete in the mid-market price range which would take on the established competition.

Rudge-Whitworth-engined motorcycles had won each race in the 1930s Isle of Man Junior TT along with first and second places in the Senior race. The Rudge engine and gearbox was sold together under the Python trade name – this was to be AJW's second choice of a winning design. The new motorcycle was named the Flying Fox and available with 350 cc or 500 cc power units. Four new 2 stroke designs and a V twin version of the Flying Fox completed the range. The Flying Fox was a successful range and sold well for over two years. AJW was by now well established in the market and profitable.

1932 The market recession was setting in. Prices had to be reduced and the AJW range was cut back. By the end of 1933 supplier Glanfield Lawrence had

Mud, gulleys, rocks and more mud! A cross country trial – number 73 is an AJW.

The AJW Flying Fox of 1933 with Python Engine

Photo: Courtesy of Roy Wheaton, Wilstead, Bedford.

gone into liquidation owing AJW Motor Company £3,000 and threatening the company with closure. Fortunately the father of a customer, Geoff Corby, offered to buy the company, an offer which was accepted, with John continuing as engineering consultant.

Arrangements were made for sales to be exclusively handled by motorcycle dealer Pride & Clarke, Stockwell Road, near Olympia. Pride & Clarke also offered their own range of 12 sidecar designs which could be fitted and colour matched to any AJW model.

1933 One hundred and sixty-one AJW motorcycles were built.

1935 The financial depression was easing. The AJW Flying Fox range was revived with a 499 cc twin-port JAP engine and 4-speed Albion gearbox. The price was £53/10s.

1936 The last series made was the Silver Vixen, initially fitted with a 495 cc Matchless single-port overhead valve engine with Burman gearbox. Later, the engine was changed to a JAP until production stopped in mid-1939. A few Villiers-powered lightweights were also built: the Standard and the deluxe Lynx.

1940s World War II started in September 1939 and continued until 2 September 1945.

In early 1940 the AJW company employed eight staff who were all called up for military service. John Wheaton and Geoff Corby closed down the business.

In their best years the AJW Motor Company made up to 250 machines annually but unconfirmed records indicated considerably more.

During the war a fire destroyed the workshop and most of the tooling jigs and remaining parts although some survived.

Alfred John Wheaton circa 1960

Above: *The AJW motorcycle workshop destroyed by fire between 1940 and 1942. The fire could have easily spread to the adjacent printing works.*

Photo: Courtesy of Owen J. Gittings, Tupsey, Hereford.

1937 Sports 500 cc with JAP engine. Renovated in 1989. This motorcycle was found rusting in a box after being stripped down in 1947.

1946 After the war, a demobbed RAF officer, Jack Ball of Bournemouth, bought the AJW name, design drawings and surviving tooling for £50.

John Wheaton had no further involvement with the AJW Motorcycle Company and joined his father Fred in the family printing and publishing business.

Jack Ball restarted production by 1949 with a new 494 cc JAP twin-cylinder side-valve engined Grey Fox model. No more than 70 machines were built after the war because sourcing of parts had become very difficult as many of the pre-war suppliers had gone out of business.

1953 The last AJW produced was a 125 cc Fox Cub priced at £91/13s /6d.

Jack Ball closed down production in Wimborne, Dorset when the JAP engine was no longer available. He then began importing Italian Minarelli lightweight machines badged as AJW. The business finally passed to a motorcycle dealer in West Drayton, Middlesex who continued importing Italian machines with Wolfhound AJW branding until about 1980.

Only about 12 to 15 of the original pre-war AJW motorcycles are known to have survived to 1996. Now in fully restored condition, some are in the Birmingham Motorcycle Museum and others are in private ownership but there must be more out there awaiting restoration.

Third from the left: *One of the several fully restored AJW motorcycles displayed at the Birmingham Motor Museum*

The offices of Pergamon Press, Oxford. Robert Maxwell's office and the boardroom are above the front entrance.

The Pergamon Era

By February 1966 terms were agreed for a merger of Wheatons with Robert Maxwell's Oxford-based Pergamon Press Ltd, publishers of scientific and academic journals and books, for a consideration of £559,500 by an issue of Pergamon shares in exchange for Wheatons.

Robert Maxwell announced expansion of the company's educational publishing programme continuing under the Wheaton imprint, together with major funding for the completion of the new factory. All 250 existing employees' jobs were secure and many new job opportunities would arise.

However, there was to be some restructuring which would emerge later.

- Educational publishing would move to Oxford, with warehousing and distribution integrated with Pergamons
- The High Street shop premises would be sold and the bookshop accommodated at 143 Fore Street
- The stationery and school supplies business, operating from Trusham Road, Marsh Barton, would continue but would be relocated adjacent to the new factory premises
- Part of the 6-acre Marsh Barton site would be sold to help finance the new factory
- Ronald Whiting and Wheaton, a recently launched but as yet unprofitable fiction book publishing imprint based in London and adding work to the factory, was to be discontinued.

John Wheaton continued as Chairman of Wheatons and joined the board of Pergamon Press. Mr Eric Buckley, joint Managing Director of Pergamon Press and Director of the Book Publishing Division joined the board of Wheatons. When John Wheaton retired, Mr Leonard Rich became Managing Director at Exeter and Anthony Wheaton was soon to be appointed to the board of Pergamon Press, later to head the Group's Printing Division of four companies.

It was very helpful to have Eric Buckley appointed to the Wheaton Board. He advised and assisted in developing relations with the Pergamon directors and staff at Oxford. Philip Dwerryhouse and Anthony Wheaton made monthly visits to Pergamon which proved very effective in forming working associations with Roy Strange, Pergamon's Production Director, and with the managers and staff of the journals and academic book publishing divisions. Reciprocal visits followed with Pergamon managers visiting Wheatons.

A progressive build up of production orders commenced with the typesetting of large format academic books. Wheatons' quarterly house journal *143* of April to August 1966 recorded that 35 titles, representing some 17,500 pages, were already in hand in the Composing Room and would soon be working through to the letterpress printing department.

In the following years, regular visits to Oxford continued and included Frank Wright and Mike Keenan as the programme grew to include scientific journals.

1967 The educational publishing department moved to Oxford. The Editorial Director, John Halsall, Sales Manager, Don Bibey, and finally some key staff agreed to move.

1968 By now the new book bindery was completed and officially opened by the Labour MP for Exeter, Mrs Gwyneth Dunwoody, with Robert Maxwell present.

Staff morale in the bindery was good. Later a group of bindery staff offered to paint, in their own time, a wall mural some 50 feet long to adorn a side wall in the bindery. The mural would depict the countryside with the rolling hills and sheep and cows in the fields to the west of Exeter where a number of the staff came from. The proposal was accepted with the company providing the materials. The mural resided in place for a number of years acting as a feel good factor and was favourably commented on by visiting customers.

The only serious competitor in the recruiting of bindery girls, aged 16, was Gossard. However, there they would just be sewing up Wonderbras all day – more variation was available at Wheatons! Personnel Training Manager Jonathon

One day you may be lucky enough...

A new factory—light, airy, spacious. Working in such pleasant surroundings could be *your* privilege. Wheatons are part of the large international publishing group, Pergamon Press, who are now in the process of building up a printing division. A. Wheaton & Co is to form the foundation of a large printing and binding plant in Exeter. They offer secure employment with ample opportunities for advancement and promotion. Rates of pay are excellent. Although vacancies are limited at present, if you are leaving school later in the year, or during the next two years, now is the time to look into the possibilities of working with this progressive company.

Write to us now. Better still, visit us for an informal talk. (Bring your parents, too, if you wish.) We will tell you something about the work we do, and we will show you round the fine new factory we have just built. Drop a line to the Works Manager at the address below. Or if you prefer to wait until nearer the time you will be leaving school, tear out this advertisement for reference. We shall be pleased to hear from you at any time in the future.

A. WHEATON & CO

A Member of the Pergamon Group

Head Office: 143 Fore Street · Exeter · Tel.: 74121

Recruitment drive. This advert was placed in the Express & Echo on 31 May 1968.

Ionides had to be more creative – he made visits to schools' careers teachers.

In the event, a final decision to commence building the printing factory was delayed by Pergamon. In the meantime printing continued at the Fore Street premises supplying the bindery at Marsh Barton.

Tribute to retiring works overseer

THE retirement on June 14 of Mr. H. W. A. E. Gubb, overseer of the bindery department of A. Wheaton & Co., printers and publishers, of Fore Street Exeter, marked the completion of 38 years' service with the company.

Mr. Gubb joined A. Wheaton & Co. in August, 1930, having previously been with the local firm of Southwood. He has held the overseer's position for the last 30 years.

Mr. John Wheaton (left), recently-retired chairman of the firm, said that Mr. Gubb had seen many changes in the bindery section during his career, from the initial small and crowded room employing some 20 men and women to a bindery four times the original size and over three times the number of staff.

In the last 12 months Mr. Gubb has been involved in the company's latest expansion programme, the new bindery at Marsh Barton Trading Estate, which is now ten times larger than the original bindery of the 1930's.

Among his many outside interests, Mr. Gubb's first love has been in the field of cage birds, which has extended over the last 45 years.

He was secretary of the South Western Cage Bird Society for 25 years, and is currently president of the South Western Border Fancy Canary Club.

Mr Gubb is also one of the top leading judges in the country in this field, having had the honour of judging no less than six times at Olympia Cage Bird Shows and most of the leading shows in the country, and has been asked to judge in Guernsey in 1969.

He has also been selected three times for the international team of exhibitors. The many cups and trophies he has won take a day to clean.

Mr. Gubb is also a keen gardener and carpentry enthusiast.

He is married, and has a married daughter.

Mr. Anthony Wheaton (director), on right, made the final presentation of a typewriter, electric drill and tools on behalf of his colleagues. Mrs. Gubb was presented with a bouquet.

1968 The retirement of Harold Gubb, overseer of the Bindery Department at Fore Street and initially at Marsh Barton, after 38 year's service with the company.

He was secretary of the South West Caged Bird Society and a national judge of canaries. As one of the most senior judges in the country in this field, he judged at Olympia shows on six occasions.

Left to right:
John Wheaton, Mrs Gubb, Harold Gubb and Anthony Wheaton

All set for a busy retirement is Mr. L. A. Rich, a director of A. Wheaton and Co., Ltd., the Exeter printing firm, who retires this week. He is seen, centre, receiving a stereophonic tape recorder and high-fi equipment from his fellow directors yesterday. They are, left to right: Messrs. P. A. Dwerryhouse, Anthony Wheaton, the managing director who made the presentation, E. Wright, and M. Pearse. Also pictured is a chest of tools given to him by the works and office staff.

The retirement of Mr L. A. Rich

On the retirement of Leonard Rich, Anthony Wheaton was appointed Managing Director of the company.

1969 A major diversion occurred. The future of Pergamon Press Group, including Wheatons, hung in the balance.

Saul Steinberg, head of Leasco Data Processing Corporation, USA, made a bid for Pergamon Press. Initially, Pergamon and Leasco announced that a sale agreement had been reached and Leasco purchased on the market 38% of Pergamon's listed shares. However, it became apparent that Pergamon's profit forecast for 1969, on which the bid price was based, was over-stated, leading to a protracted dispute between the parties.

Pergamon's shares were suspended on the London Stock Market. In October 1969, the board of Pergamon, including Robert Maxwell, was removed from office on a shareholders' poll vote.

An enquiry by the Department of Trade and Industry under the City Takeover Code at the time took until mid-1971 to produce an interim report and until 1973 to produce a final report totalling 1,243 pages. The report concluded that 'Maxwell had contrived to maximise Pergamon's share price through transactions between his private family companies'.

At the same time a US Congress enquiry was critical of Leasco's practices in their bid process. Litigation followed between Pergamon Press, Oxford (now Leasco controlled) and Pergamon Press Inc. USA (still in the control of Maxwell now residing in the USA).

In November three previous Pergamon Directors including Anthony Wheaton accepted invitations to rejoin the board and were appointed to work with the Americans who, of course, had no operating knowledge of the Group companies.

The new Chairman of Pergamon appointed by financial institutions and major shareholders was Sir Henry d'Avigdor-Goldsmid and, on 30 January 1970, Dr Felix Kalinski from the USA was appointed Group Managing Director. Later, Sir Walter Coutts became Chairman.

1969 The integration of Wheatons' Educational Publishing Department within Pergamon in Oxford was not a success.

In so far as sales and distribution were concerned the move proved to be a complete disaster. Despite the assurances given that facilities for distribution of specimen copies were available, no such department did in fact exist. This was an essential requirement for an educational publisher. Despite Wheatons' Sales Manager's repeated requests,

The retirement presentation to George Lyndall, with his wife, after operating Smyth-Horne case-making and book casing-in bindery machinery at Fore Street since the 1950s. The presentation was made at Marsh Barton in about 1970 by John Wheaton (seen here with his wife Doris) after his own retirement.

no co-operation was given and as a result sales representatives' requests for specimen copies had to be routed through the warehouse as individual orders. Since this resulted in delays of anything up to three weeks, by the time the teachers received the requested specimen books they were useless.

Wheatons' overseas agents who were well known and respected by head teachers in their own territories had now to fill out time-consuming paperwork returns to Pergamon. In spite of the fact that they were now far better paid at Pergamon than they had ever been at Wheatons, one by one they left to take other jobs. The only contribution made by Pergamon's Export Manager was to cancel contracts with Wheatons' old established agents in such places as Canada, Australia, New Zealand and Malaya and to appoint in their place Pergamon agents who had not the slightest knowledge or interest in the Wheaton list.

The situation on the distribution side was even worse. No advance assessment had been made before the move of the difference between handling orders in bulk quantities as Wheatons' consignments often were and the more or less one off sales of the academic books published by the Pergamon Book Division. The result was that the capacity of the warehouse bins was far too small and an otherwise efficient layout was unable to cope with this new situation. Orders which had previously taken a week to process in Exeter were now taking up to a month, resulting in very serious complaints, particularly from the large school book contractors.

Much damage was done to Wheatons' reputation both in the trade and in the schools themselves during the first year or so.

1970 Under Leasco's stewardship, a strategic review was undertaken of all Group companies to identify those key to the core business needs of Pergamon. Wheatons, a profitable business, by now the main Group printer with a staff of 280 and producing 48% of the academic book production needs and 25% of the learned journals, survived this review. Some other Group subsidiaries were sold off or identified for sale.

In 1970 Pergamon Press published for NASA the *Proceedings of the Apollo 11 Lunar Science Conference*, following the successful manned mission to the moon in July 1969. The proceedings and other NASA material ran to some 7,000 pages of scientific text and micro-analysis half-tones of the moon rock samples. The typesetting was undertaken by EPC and the University Press Belfast. The three-volume set had however to be printed in the USA rather than by Wheatons as had been hoped.

1971 A single copy warehouse department was set up at Wolverton near Oxford to specifically cater for educational publishing and for some other non-Group publishers now using Pergamon's service. Overall, the warehousing service was now satisfactory to Wheatons.

1972 A concerted effort was made from Wheatons to obtain approval to complete the building of the new factory. Anthony Wheaton prepared a report showing how if Group journal and book formats could be standardised with agreement of the journal editors, and the range of papers reduced, considerable production cost savings would accrue to the Group.

Continued on page 58

The Marsh Barton factory under construction. *The bindery on the left was built first and was operating by 1972. The printed sheet warehouse and journals bindery at the rear is also completed. The printing factory to the foreground is completed but the office block is still under construction.*

Note the one metre drop from road level in undeveloped areas of the site. The front half of the warehouse to the rear and across the road was later rented by the company.

About **Robert Maxwell**

Robert Maxwell was born Ján Ludvík Hyman Binyamin Hoch to a Jewish family in Czechoslovakia, close to the Russian border, in 1923. He escaped from Nazi occupation of the country in 1939 working his way, sometimes as a paperboy, across Europe to France. He eventually joined the British Army having adopted the pseudonym Du Maurier.

By 1945 the multi-lingual Du Maurier became Robert Maxwell on the Army's advice. By now he had become a lieutenant in the North Staffordshire Regiment and then joined the Queen's Royal Regiment (West Surrey) which had been involved in actions across Europe to Berlin. By the end of the war he had been promoted to the rank of Captain. He won a Military Cross for a heroic action in Holland in January 1945 and was decorated by Field Marshal Montgomery.

After the liberation of Paris he met his future wife, Elisabeth Meynard from Lyon, who was acting as an interpreter with the French Welcome Committee.

Top left: *Captain Robert Maxwell MC. He later joined the Queen's Royal Regiment (West Surrey).*
Above: *Robert Maxwell with his wife at home in Headington Hill Hall Oxford*

Above: *A Military Cross. The MC was awarded to Robert Maxwell by Field Marshall Montgomery.*

They went on to have seven children.

At the end of the war Robert Maxwell was posted to the British Control Commission in Berlin, one of the Allied departments administering Germany. This job, in the Press Section as a Control Commission Officer, involved commercial licensing and news production and brought him in contact with influential officials, European publishers and Russian officials. After the war, with an associate, Dr Paul Rosbaud (a scientific editor), they acquired a majority interest in Butterworth Springer – a scientific publisher. Before the war, Springer had been a small scientific publisher in West Berlin. Maxwell's knowledge of regulation and export procedures emerging from the chaos in Europe after the war was to prove an invaluable benefit. Later they renamed the company Pergamon Press and based it in London. Later still the headquarters were established in Oxford.

Pergamon was to become a major European and international scientific and academic publisher.

Robert Maxwell at the the launch of Wheatons' 'Crown Reading Scheme' in London in 1980.

With Maxwell's wartime contacts in Europe and the Soviet Union, the intelligence services of western governments suspected that he may have operated as an agent. The FBI in America spent years monitoring Maxwell's movements and contacts but found no evidence that he was trading secrets.

Robert Maxwell entered politics and served as Labour MP for Buckinghamshire from October 1964 to January 1970. In Parliament he was put in charge of the Commons' Catering Committee.

He was various addressed – by the media as Cap'n Bob, Mr Maxwell by his staff, Chairman at board meetings and Bob by his close associates. Amongst company colleagues he was known as IRM. However, if he referred to you as Mr – it was time to look out!

Robert Maxwell died in suspicious circumstances in 1991. He is buried on the Mount of Olives in Jerusalem and was given almost a state funeral by Israel. ✡

Continued from page 54

With new plant added such standardisation could be achieved at Wheatons by a batch production approach on two mini-web offset presses and using flowline binding methods.

The report showing the investment required and significant financial benefits over the next five years was approved by the board.

A further proposal also approved was to set up a journal back issue warehouse whereby single copy dispatches of previously published issues and off print articles were order processed and mailed daily worldwide.

No time was lost in completing the planning and building of the new printing factory and offices totalling 108,000 square feet, including accommodation for Educational Publishing and for Wheatons' thriving Sports & Social Club. Anthony Wheaton with main contractor, N Pratt & Co, coordinated some 20 sub-contractors. These included Matthews Electrical Company – often called back in following years to upgrade the wiring as more machines were added.

1973 The new factory and warehouses were completed at a cost of some £300,000.

The factory complex included a bungalow for the company's Chief Engineer, Cyril Steer, who then lived in the premises as caretaker. Also included was a sub-branch of Barclays Bank to serve the company and the Marsh Barton community.

A further £308,000 investment was made in new Comprite computer typesetting plant and production machinery, with more investment later.

Installed in the new office entrance foyer was a Greig–Columbian platen printing press as link with the past. The ancient press, originally acquired in 1906 and used by the company up to 1926 to print posters from wooden type, had remained abandoned in a courtyard at Fore Street for over 40 years. At a cost of £700 the press was restored to full working order by printer's engineer, Harry F Rochat. Painted in traditional black, the large eagle at the top of the press frame was part gold leafed.

The Greig–Columbian platen press

In 1987 BPCC was to consider that the antique press did not portray a sufficiently modern image at the entrance to the company, and after 14 years on display, the press was sold.

After completion of the new factory, the site and premises were sold by Pergamon Press to Metropolitan Estates & Property Co (MEPC) and leased back.

The Wheatons' Fore Street property was eventually sold for £120,000 for housing development following some years attempting to gain planning approval from Exeter City Council.

1972–3 Pergamon's stewardship under Leasco proved to be somewhat of a holding position without much progress made in terms of overall Group development and profitability.

1974 Robert Maxwell, with new funding from US backers, made a successful bid and regained control of Pergamon Press.

There was some apprehension as to how Maxwell would react when the first board meeting under his Chairmanship took place. However, he was generally appreciative of the efforts of the three original board members in holding the Group together during the five year interregnum.

It was agreed with the Pergamon Board that Wheatons' Educational Publishing Department should return to Exeter together with the Religious and Moral Education Press imprint. The editorial team was also to be rebuilt. In June 1974 John Halsall returned to Exeter with just six staff. A condition however was that educational book order processing and dispatch would remain at the Pergamon Group warehouse at Wolverton.

The Comprite photo typesetting system for technical text was upgraded with Monotype Lasercomp 600 film setters. Metal typesetting was phased out. The Composing Department now employed 77 typesetters, page makeup and proof reading staff.

By June 1974 the new factory was completed and equipped. Robert Maxwell made a tour of the factory with the Mayor and Mayoress of Exeter. Maxwell had not visited Exeter since the opening of the new bindery in 1969, during the intervention years of the Leasco affair. He was anxious to make up for lost time with ambitious plans for Pergamon's expansion but there was to be trouble ahead for UK industry and the economy.

Continued on page 62

The official opening of the Marsh Barton bindery as reported by The Express & Echo *on Friday, 31 May 1969.*
Left to Right: *Mrs Gwyneth Dunwoody, MP for Exeter; Anthony Wheaton, Managing Director; Robert Maxwell, Chairman and Managing Director of Pergamon Press Ltd and Frank Wright, Works Director.*

NEW BINDERY FOR A. WHEATON & CO., EXETER

FROM LEFT: Mrs. Gwyneth Dunwoody, M.P. for Exeter, Mr. Anthony J. Wheaton (a director of Pergamon Press Ltd. and joint manager of the printing division), Mr. Robert Maxwell, M.P. (chairman and managing director of Pergamon Press Ltd.), and Mr. F. H. Wright (works manager, A. Wheaton and Co.) at the official opening of the new bindery.

From patent pills to publishing

(BY PATRICIA AVERY AND MICHAEL PASSMORE)

LAST Friday saw the opening in Exeter of a new £200,000 book bindery for A. Wheaton and Company, the local firm of printers, publishers, and booksellers. The occasion marked the completion of the first phase of an expansion plan for the six-acre site recently acquired by the company — a development which will provide considerable additional capacity for letterpress and lithographic printing and book-binding.

This will enable the company to offer increased services to publishers and commercial customers and to undertake a greater proportion of the production of journals and books published by the Pergamon Press Group, with whom Wheaton's merged some two years ago.

But Wheaton's were not always the printing, publishing, and bookselling firm well known in the city in latter years. In Old Moore's Almanack for 1844 many of the advertisements were for patent medicines sold by Wheaton's in their small bookshop near the top of Fore Street.

Here were Antibilious Pills, Pennyroyal Fennole Pills, Magic Pills for Curing Gout, and, in case a possible market had been overlooked, Enowey's Pills "to cure all complaints."

Side by side with the pill-boxes, however, were the educational books which were to form the basis of Wheaton's future trading. The 1844 edition of Old Moore's Almanack also included advertisements for Wheaton's school books, "Spellings, Gramers, Exercises, Psalters, Tutors, Assistants, Catechisms, and a large stock of Juvenile books—entertaining and instructive."

Thus the small retail bookshop was already on its way to greater things, and in 1906 the limited company of A Wheaton was incorporated.

In the same year, a small printing firm in Exeter were taken over so that Wheaton's could begin to print the work they were already publishing.

Destined to grow

The small firm whom the directors decided to acquire was to form the nucleus of the printing side of the business—a department destined to expand beyond their wildest dreams. The premises consisted of a small building at the corner of Preston Street.

Work at that time was chiefly concerned with the production of labels, magazines, and general trade printing, in addition to satisfying the requirements of the publishing department. Business flourished, particularly the latter, and the printshop was soon outgrown.

The need for larger premises was evident, and solved by the purchase of property in Fore Street which which being vacated by the Western Times Company. This, still in use, was added to over the years by the purchase of adjoining buildings and new construction, until the Wheaton printworks and administrative offices occupied some 66,000 square feet. Trade continued to expand, and exports to many parts of the world built up as Wheaton books were adopted throughout the educational field.

The fairly consistent growth rate continued right up until the middle 1960's, when the technological revolution in the printing industry caused the company to take stock of their position within the trade. Printers were beginning to regroup themselves into large and powerful combines, and were thus able to equip themselves with the very complex and expensive machinery of this computer age.

It became obvious that within the next 5 to 10 years the industry would be dramatically transformed. There was likely to be a small number of large companies and a large number of very small units, with no place for the middle-sized printer, who would thus be forced to merge or be squeezed out of existence.

Merger decision

The directors, therefore, decided to merge with someone of common interests. Robert Maxwell's publishing organisation, Pergamon Press, were anxious to enter the educational book market at school level—a field in which Wheaton's were specialists. Robert Maxwell was also interested in acquiring a printworks on which to build a printing division. Here then was the ideal merger. The publishing department became the sole responsibility of Pergamon Press in Oxford and Wheaton's Exeter factory ... become the headquarters

A section of the new bindery

Firm's expansion held up by housing shortage

A shortage of key workers was holding up expansion of one of the Westcountry's biggest printing firms, said the publisher and ex-Labour M.P., Mr Robert Maxwell, at Exeter yesterday

The chairman of Pergamon Press Ltd., and millionaire socialist Mr. Maxwell said that there were many new machines standing idle at the Marsh Barton factory of A. Wheaton and Company because there were not the skilled people in Exeter to handle them.

This was causing loss of production and in a delay in meeting export orders to a company which had expanded substantially in the last eight years. Skilled man-power could be obtained from different parts of the country but workers could not take up jobs because of lack of housing.

Mr. Maxwell said he had had discussions with the council and particularly with the chairman of the housing committee who understood what the needs of the company were. He was very impressed by the new administration in Exeter and hoped the council would take positive action. The local authorities would have to provide housing accommodation for key workers.

Rampant inflation

Mr. Maxwell was speaking to representatives of a hundred publishers from all over the country during his second visit to the factory since it had been in full production.

Wheaton's, he said, employed 400 people at the moment but could provide jobs for another 200 after further expansion. Thirty women were needed now.

In 1966 when Wheaton's merged with Pergamon Press the firm was employing 250 people.

The new factory, a bright modern and clean building covering six acres, cost £350,000 to build and contains new machinery worth more than £1m. The family business, which started in the 1900s deals with religious, educational and children's books and prints over 10,000,000 books a year, including 1,000 new titles.

Mr. Maxwell, former M.P. for Buckingham, said tremendous damage was being done to the country by rampant inflation 'from which we were all suffering'. He warned: 'I assure you the country is riding to destruction unless the Government gets to grips with the disastrous rate of inflation'.

Rates had gone up by 35% in comparison with six months ago, boards for binding by 300%, paper by 100% and fuel-oil by 236%.

Must roll up sleeves

If the rate of inflation were allowed to continue it would bring to end the political democracy and freedom 'of the kind we have enjoyed in centuries and have come to expect as our birthright'.

'Unless, ' said Mr. Maxwell, 'we all roll up our sleeves it will surely destroy us.'

He hoped the Labour Government would be re-elected with a working majority soon. A minority government was not in a position to cope with inflation.

Mr. Maxwell congratulated Mr. Anthony Wheaton, Managing Director of the firm and great-grandson of its founder, on making the factory one of the most modern book and journal printing factories in Europe.

After he had been shown around the factory he said Wheaton's work as printers and publishers had carried the name of Exeter all over the world.

He said: 'My impression is that the factory is first-rate. I have very high expectations for the people working here. The future progress and prosperity of Wheaton's will continue to make a substantial contribution to the welfare of Exeter and industrial expansion.'

The Mayor and Mayoress of Exeter, Mr. Sam Honeywill and Mrs. Kathleen le Milliere, also toured the factory.

Friends and relatives of employees were able to have a look around the factory today. ■

During the 1970s, Jackie Ford operated the first GPO PBX telephone switchboard that was installed in the reception at the Marsh Barton Factory.

Continued from page 59

1975 The phasing out of Monotype and Intertype metal typesetting and the Letterpress Printing Department proceeded over several years and was completed in 1975 after occupation of the new factory. During this period 'repro pulls' were taken on heavy grammage matt art paper at the commencement of each letterpress-printed reprint from metal type (all new work being thereafter film set for lithographic printing). 'Repro pulls' were carefully made-ready best quality printed sheets to include all pages in an edition. These sheets were then photographed to negative film on the company's Littlejohn gallery process camera. The film was then subsequently used to make litho plates for the next editions.

Wheatons had an historical archive of several hundred tons of standing bookwork in type-page form. As titles were converted to film the type pages were melted down, cast to ingots and sold on the metal market. The sale proceeds significantly helped to fund new plant purchases.

1973–79 Over this period national inflation ran at an astonishing average of 18%, peaking at 25% in 1975.

Trade Union wage increases (including print unions) did not keep pace with price increases leading to industrial unrest and in 1974 'the summer of discontent'.

Following the National Union of Mineworkers (NUM) conference vote in 1973 for a 35% wage increase, the government introduced capping controls on wages. The NUM strike followed and with reduced power station output, the government imposed a three-day working week throughout industry from 1 January to 7 March 1974.

Power generators became impossible to source in the UK. Wheatons obtained two units (one from Germany) and installed these to produce sufficient

The administration department's office party, 1973

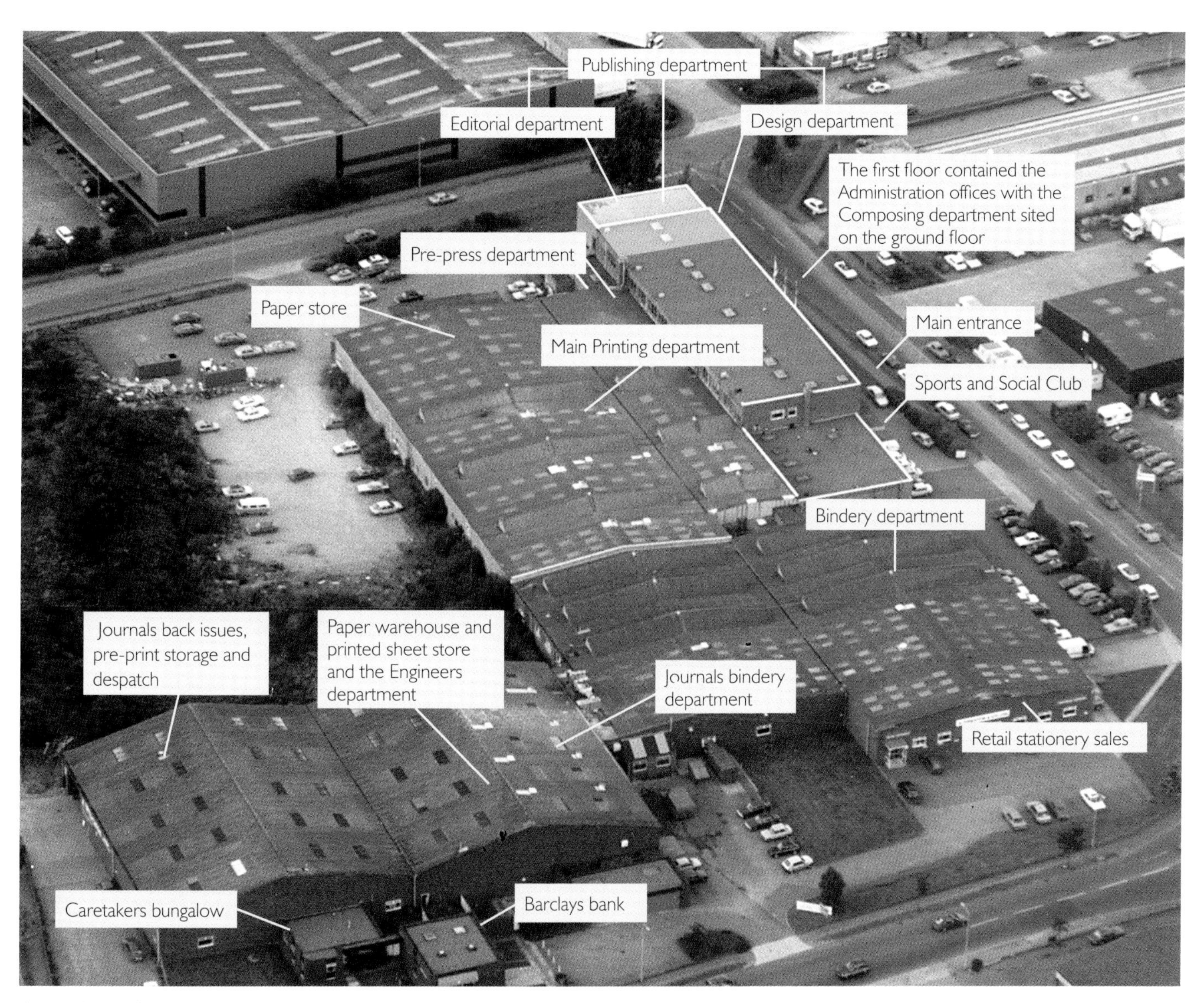

An aerial view of the Marsh Barton factory after its completion in 1974

1970s Sports Club Awards

Left to right: *Cyril Steer, David Lee and Anthony Wheaton*

Left to right: *Myrtle Lee and Anthony Wheaton*

power on 'off days' to maintain five-day working.

The single phase and three phase power available enabled typesetting, key printing and the binding plant to keep operating. It was possible to maintain schedules for the Pergamon journal programme and other customers' date-sensitive publications throughout this period.

The company's most successful Sales Director – Mike Keenan, was appointed Managing Director of the printing company.

Between 1975 and 1989 the company operated a small production unit to make litho printing plates within a government-designated Assisted Development Area. A production unit was set up at Burrington in mid-Devon and later moved to Ivybridge near Plymouth when the boundary of the development area was revised. Commercial activity in the development areas were grant assisted.

1976 At this time Wheatons were manufacturing in the order of 10 million books and publications per annum from almost 100 publishers.

A frequent visitor was Eric Green, driver of the Pergamon Press 20-ton lorry, collecting Group books for delivery to the Pergamon warehouse at Wolverton near Oxford.

As Wheatons was the main Group printing facility, Robert Maxwell, as Chairman of Wheatons, resumed a close interest in the development of the company, regularly chairing board meetings at Exeter and sometimes settling disputes with the unions.

Robert Maxwell rarely travelled by train. Prior to his visits all parked cars had to be cleared from the entrance area for the arrival of the Rolls Royce driven by chauffeur Claude Hoppit.

Working relations with Chairman Robert Maxwell were not always cordial. Tactics were applied in some years to suppress Wheatons' earnings, perhaps to quell the aspirations of the unions. This would be implemented by applying Group charges in the accounts, partly justified by making educational book stock value adjustments.

In 1980 a 10% discount was applied as a 'one off' for the Pergamon Book Publishing Division. In some years price increases on Group work were restricted to well below the national rate of inflation. Such measures, coupled with the replacement of Wheatons' long-standing staff pension scheme by the less beneficial Pergamon Group Scheme, caused dismay among senior staff.

Another concern for senior staff was that salaries had been subject to a government national wage restraint policy limiting salary increases to a maximum of £208 in the year 1974 whereas factory staff benefitted from higher national union pay increases.

When cost cutting exercises were negotiated between local management and unions but not finally resolved, Maxwell would come down to Exeter to 'conclude matters'. He would insist on seeing the 'Fathers of the Chapels' (FOCs) by themselves, introducing himself as an 'impartial friend' to help them through this stage. He would often concede to the FOCs over half of the points which management had been holding out for. With their authority reduced, management were in an invidious position next time there was a dispute.

To offset lower price increases from the Group, Wheatons were encouraged to build up more non-Group work. At this time Pergamon's book publishing programme was cut back resulting in less Group work available for Exeter.

Managing Sales Director, Mike Keenan, very successfully built up new accounts with London area publishers over the next few years.

There were, however, helpful encouragements for productivity and efficiency improvements in staff departments which were largely non-union.

In 1976 a Pergamon Group staff pay and conditions review took place putting in place a bonus scheme from which Wheatons' staff were to benefit. The scheme was not in breach of the government's pay policy at the time (maximum increase in salary of £208 per annum). Staff would benefit as long as the company continued to earn profits during the year.

Bonus awards were to be at the discretion of the directors (of Wheatons) and dependent on recommendations from elected staff representatives in each administrative section. The bonuses, paid in two installments, could be up to a maximum of 6 months' salary. Most staff benefitted to some extent.

When there were announcements to be made to factory staff Robert Maxwell would have two pallets to stand upon positioned in the machine room of the Printing Department and have the employees assembled. Taking a tip from his time as a Labour MP for Bletchley (1964–1970), he would ask quietly for the names of two employees, one at the front and one at the back of the assembly. He would start the meeting with a shrill two-fingered whistle for attention. Later he would point to a selected employee, addressing them by their Christian name and ask a question. The whole assembly would be alert and listening after that – expecting that anyone could be next!

It was usually difficult to have sufficient time with Maxwell to discuss a proposal or obtain a decision on matters. Therefore, the best approach was to arrange to see him at his office in Headington Hill, Oxford early on a Saturday or a Sunday morning. He was usually in his office from 4 or 5 a.m. to speak to overseas Group companies. One had to be aware, however, that the conversation was probably being recorded (a microphone was discovered under a table lamp adjacent to the visitor's chair).

The main entrance to Pergamon Press and Headington Hill Hall, Oxford

Such visits on Sundays could lead on to an invitation to stay for lunch which would involve dining with invited MPs, national business figures and perhaps a celebrity or two. A large teddy bear was always sat on chair number 13.

In September 1976 joint Managing Director Frank Wright left the company after 22 years but he re-joined in 1978.

1977 In November a long-service recognition reception was held at an Exeter restaurant. Twenty-nine members of the company's staff were congratulated and thanked for their service ranging from 25 to 50 years. See the employees long serving listing on page 68.

The company was restructured into three operating and profit centres reporting to Anthony Wheaton as Executive Deputy Chairman as shown below.

Print production

(Including typesetting and binding) with joint Managing Directors
Mike Keenan (sales) and **Frank Wright** (production)

Publishing under Publishing Director
John Halsall

School and Commercial Supplies Director
Edgar Andrews

Finance Director
Michael Pearce

General Office and Accounts Manager
Eric Luffman

The Printing Company management

Production Manager
David Miller

Works Administrative Manager and Technical Manager
Alan Shaw

Composing Department Manager
Ron Buckingham

Printing Department Manager
Ken Baker
(including litho plate making department and paper warehouse)

Bindery Managers
Bill Payne and **Mike Hawker**
(including printed sheet warehouse and journals back issue service)

Chief Maintenance Engineer
Cyril Steer

The Book Plan Diary

The Book Plan was a cost effective, standard format and materials production service for publishers. The Plan included pricing look up tables ranging from 500 to 10,000 copies in paginations from 96pp to 544pp. The Plan became popular with the smaller to medium size general book publishers. Published as a Diary, with the planned specification and prices at the front, it was issued annually to all publisher customers and potential customers with suitable work.

The 'Book Plan' service was launched providing a pre-costed, standard format and paper, print and bind service to general publishers. This popular service ran for over 12 years and, by 1987, had built up to sales of over £1million per annum.

The Pergamon Commonwealth and International Library series of 1,000 titles was placed with the company together with Robert Maxwell's Leaders of the World bibliographical series.

Wheatons had now become a major producer of Group journals – the most profitable and important part of Pergamon's publishing programme. It was decided that the Journals Division should have its own 'forward post' at Exeter. A separate Journals Production Control (JPU) section was set up within Wheatons' Production Department with Pergamon employee Peter Grooms in charge.

The section operated a colour-coded card system showing the receipt date of each issue and subsequently its location in factory departments and due completion date. The cards were mounted on rails on A-frame racks to show all work in progress updated several times a day. Later, Wheatons' staff joined the JPU section and it became a larger computer-based information monitoring department.

International bulk mailing of journals was conducted from the bindery. The company negotiated a discount on business postal rates for pre-sorting addresses into international zip codes. Racks of post office sacks were filled daily and collected by the post office. The sacks were sealed and only opened for addressee final delivery of individual copies once in the zip code overseas post office location.

With the benefits of the new working practices coming to fruition, and non-Group sales to 90 UK publishers now running at 40% of turnover, Wheatons returned an operating profit (pre-Group charges and tax) of £531,000 for the 1978 trading year, of which £126,000 arose from educational publishing.

The factory required additional warehouse space for a part-bound book and flat-printed-sheet store, so a 20,000 square feet extension was added adjacent to the bindery. Later,

Long Service Reception for Wheatons' employees

18 November 1977

Name	Title	Years of Service
Mr Ken Baker	Machine Room Manager	34
Mr Bill Court	Journals Issues Controller	32
Mr Edgar Dolling	Composing Room Stonehand	48
Mr Derek Ellis	Camera Room Overseer	34
Mr Tony Ellis	Bindery Supervisor	25
Miss Sheila Elsworthy	Bindery Packer	27
Mr Frank Grimes	Machine Manager	25
Mrs Chris Guppy	Bonus Clark	47
Mr Roy James	Guillotine Operator	35
Mr Cyril Laythorpe	Machine Manager	39
Mr Fred Lee	Machine Manager	50
Mr Ern Litton	Filmsetter/Computer Operator	43
Mr Lionel Lovell	Journals Production Co-ordinator	38
Mr Trevor Luffman	Account Executive	30
Mr George Lydall	Bindery Overseer	29
Miss Pat Marshall	Machine Room Assistant	29
Miss Margaret Murphy	Senior Costing Clerk	27
Mr Cyril Napper	Plateroom Storeman	50
Mr Harold Palfrey	Film Make-up	28
Mr Arthur Payne	Casemaker	31
Mr Ron Pengilly	Folding Machine Assistant	29
Mrs Gloria Perkins	Retail: Textbook Supervisor	34
Mr George Pope	Plateroom Storeman	43
Mr Rod Ryell	Compositor	32
Mr John Seccombe	Publishing Manager	27
Mr Ken Skinner	Senior Journals Issue Controller *(Non Group)*	41
Mr Philip Smale	Guillotine Operator	40
Mr Rodney Taylor	Film Make-up	27
Mr Dick Williams	Machine Room Overseer	28

Also Present

Guests now in Retirement

Mr J Wheaton	Past Chairman
Mr H Gubb	Bindery Manager *(Retired 14.6.68)*
Mr N Brown	Machine Room Manager *(Retired 3.3.68)*

Directors and Managers

Mr I R Maxwell	Chairman
Mr A J Wheaton	Deputy Chairman
Mr M Keenan	Managing Director
Mr M J Pearce	Financial Director
Mr J Halsall	Publishing Director
Mr E J Andrews	Retail Director
Mr A Shaw	Production and Technical Manager
Mr E Luffman	Office Manager
Mr R Buckingham	Composing Room Manager
Mr W Pain	Bindery Manager
Mr J L Ionides	Personnel and Training Manager
Mrs D Dickson	PA to Deputy Chairman

further flat printed sheet and bound book warehousing space was rented on the other side of the road adjacent to the bindery.

1978 Pergamon had earlier acquired a technical typesetting company in Dublin called Graphic Films, from Lord Thompson of Thompson Newspaper Group, Canada. This company was renamed the European Printing Company (EPC) with a view to Pergamon expanding in Ireland at a time when there were attractive government training grants and tax breaks for incoming companies. EPC, with a staff of 120, was re-equipped with the same technical typesetting facilities as Wheatons.

In addition to typesetting for US and Dutch publishers, EPC also undertook a progressive build up of Pergamon journal typesetting. These journals were then printed at Exeter, bringing the total printed there to some 160 monthly, bi-monthly and quarterly titles, representing 45% of Pergamon's Journal Division programme.

In the meantime, Pergamon went on to acquire E J Arnold of Leeds – another long established educational publishing company who printed their own titles in addition to manufacturing school exercise books and commercial stationery.

Both companies were later integrated to form new imprint Arnold-Wheaton.

However, not to repeat the problems Wheatons encountered at Oxford, Arnolds continued to publish from Leeds.

It was arranged that all educational book production from both imprints would be placed at Exeter. Amid some contention, Arnolds large format Roland 800 4-colour lithographic press was moved to Exeter to cope with the volume and became Wheatons' second move into serious colour printing.

The following article (pages 70–75) published by *Printing World*, in May 1978 and produced as a pull-out feature, gives a window on the printing company's activities and services at this time.

Continued on page 76

1978 London: *Mike Keenan making the presentation of a leather bound copy of the most Reverend Bruno Heim's book of English Heraldry.* 'Heraldry in the Catholic Church – its Origins, Customs and Laws' *was printed at Wheatons.*

The Most Reverend Bruno Heim was the Vatican's first Apostolic Nuncio to Britain.

Production-line printing pays

After a decision had been made to leave the old site in the city centre for a new factory on the Marsh Barton Trading Estate on the outskirts of Exeter, it was announced that A. Wheaton & Co were to merge with Pergamon Press Ltd. This led to a more ambitious redevelopment plan and the first stage of the new plant, the bindery, opened in 1968.

Five-colour Crabtree Sovereign press

A warehouse for storage of printed sheets was soon added and in 1973 the move was completed, leaving only a bookshop in the town centre.

The new building and the services Wheatons can offer are bound together. The factory, together with account handling and production control offices have been designed on the flow-line principle and it is the exploitation of this which has shaped the company's commercial policy.

Basically what Wheatons offer are two systems for producing either journals or books to a standard format at a very low cost.

The company are keen to point out however that the economies possible with standardization do not mean uniformity of product. With the impressive range of equipment at the Marsh Barton site they can in fact produce a very wide range of final products, without forfeiting the advantages of their system.

At the heart of the system are three mini-web presses. But the story begins with the setting operation which is heavily orientated towards complex technical setting which they see as an expanding market for the future.

Printing World, May 1978

In Exeter the system is tailored round a Comprite computer and three Monophoto 600 photosetters.

Inputting into these are the Monotype 600 justifying keyboards, 14 Monotype 913 keyboards, and a Compugraphic justifying keyboard.

Work is split according to complexity between the various keyboards with the more difficult mathematical setting going through the 600s.

The battery of 913 keyboards produce unjustified copy which is processed in the Comprite computer. This has a disc system on which the justified information is stored. This can be retrieved for editing and correction on VDT's.

The company have a sister organization, The European Printing Corporation, in the Group operating outside Dublin.

Their set-up is based on two Linotron 505C's with 40 input keyboards. They are also technical setting specialists, providing a service for UK, European and American book and journal publishers.

When they want to use the printing and binding services, film pages are flown direct from Dublin to Exeter, giving a fast service.

One of Wheaton's visual display terminals

Comprite computer used for justifying and storing text

Trade Magazine **Article**

The European Printing Corporation was set up in 1964 with the support of the Irish Government. They now set more than 50 learned journals a year covering a range of scientific, mathematical and technical subjects. The Dublin-based company also has an editorial team and an artwork department equipped to produce line illustrations and diagrams from author's roughs.

The Linotron 505C is a computer-controlled photosetter with a sophisticated mathematical setting programme.

It can also deal with chemical formulae and foreign language setting, and be used to output hard copy or film for information updating and retrieval or to set computer-stored information such as directories and price lists. It also enables indices to be compiled automatically for insertion at the end of a volume.

Back at Exeter, output from the photosetters can be processed by conventional camera plate making methods or by one of the few 3M Pyrofax systems in the UK.

This consists of two units, and Imager and a Fuser. They provide a very cheap, lightly grained litho plate up to A1 size which is good for runs up to 100,000 on the web presses. Quality is good for test and line illustrations but for screens finer than about 80 conventional plate making methods are used. The conventional camera department is well equipped with Kodak, Littlejohn, Multichrome and Pictorial apparatus.

There is also a vestigial hot-metal capability which is soon to be removed. It consists of one Monotype keyboard and three Monotype casters feeding a considerably slimmed-down Letterpress department used mainly for top quality text work, though Wheatons believe that the same quality can be achieved with the modern offset equipment used.

The cleanliness and order ruling in the press room are symptoms of the company's systematic approach to printing. White paper comes in from a giant warehouse at one end of the shop, trolleys have ample gangways to move through and the presses are arranged to fit in with the flow-line concept. Printed sheets, both flat and folded move straight through to the bindery on one of two routes according to the finishing process to be applied, or to the printed paper warehouse.

A formidable battery of printing machinery occupies the press room. As in the origination section of the plant a policy of duplication has been applied.

The reason is explained by managing director Mike Keenan: "The major through-put area we have had to study has been duplication. It has been necessary to ensure that a break-down anywhere along the line would not bring the whole operation to a halt."

At the front of the room are the letterpress machines, four Heidelbergs and a quad demy Miehle, these too are due to go soon.

Beyond them are the new litho presses which turn out by far the bulk of the printed material.

At the centre of the operation are three mini-webs – two single unit Harris-Marinonis and one double unit Cottrell Marinoni. They are all cold-set webs but quality is high and about 95 per cent of the journals printed at Wheatons come off the webs.

Specially high-quality work such as plates for medical journals is printed on sheet-fed machines and bound in later.

It is with the web presses that the benefits of a standardized format really start to pay off in a startling way. Very

Marinoni two-unit mini-web

short runs become viable as changeover from one journal to another take a matter of only a few minutes.

Plate change-overs take on average only six minutes and in most cases other adjustments to the presses are not necessary.

To attain this, Wheatons offer a limited choice of papers that they say are suitable for most journals. They are bought in bulk giving a considerable saving and avoiding many supply problems.

One of the webs in used for printing books on Wheaton's fixed price Book Plan.

This applies to the philosophy behind the journal printing operation to book printing, offering low fixed prices to publishers if they conform to certain format restrictions.

Under the plan two papers are offered, an 85gsm and an 80gsm Dartex paper. Extensive stocks of these are kept by the company in standard 888mm reel widths and either paper can be chosen without varying the fixed price offered because of the advantages of bulk buying.

Using standard papers and standard formats, runs as short as 1,000 copies are economically worthwhile. Two binding styles are offered either flexi-cover or hard case.

The Book Plan has proved very popular among general and educational publishers in particular, but Wheatons are by no means restricted to this kind of production. Some of their work goes to the opposite end of the complexity scale with projects such as educational kits – folders containing wide range of printed matter in all sizes, colours and forms.

Backing up the immensely productive web units are a range of sheet fed-presses. The largest press in the park is a Five unit Crabtree Sovereign. This is extensively used for Children's picture books and the extra printing unit offers the kind of advantages to publishers in which Wheatons specialize.

Many of the books printed on the Sovereign are international editions, requiring text in more than one language. When this is the requirement two units are used for the text colour,

Trade Magazine **Article**

usually black. When the changeover from one language to another is made only one unit needs to be changed.

Another service for publishers is linked to the company's extensive warehousing facilities.

When a decision has not been made about the number of copies to be printed in each language, the full colour work can be completed and the sheets stored to be finished later, probably on one of Wheaton's two Mann NP56 Perfectors.

Wheatons also have two two-colour Roland Ultra 6 presses which are compatible with the Sovereign and the Manns, giving them the back-up which is a target throughout the plant.

Completing the line-up are two Heidelberg Kords and a Crabtree Falcon U2/26.

These are used mostly for covers and plates but they give the company greater flexibility and great depth of cover in case of breakdowns.

It is in the bindery that the most recent developments have taken place. The standard journal production scheme and the Book Plan put great weight on the finishing department to provide variety.

Latest acquisition is a Kolbus Compact 32 line. This gives Wheatons what they claim to be one of the most modern automated hard case binding capabilities and its capacity is such that they can offer a trade service as well as servicing the material printed by themselves.

Finishing equipment includes machinery from Kolbus, Smyth and Muller Martini including a Martini Norm binder with a sixteen-station gatherer and an automatic six-station gatherer, stitcher, trimmer with a cover feed for saddle stich work.

On Book Plan, thread sewing in 16-page sections is offered as an alternative to perfect binding at a small extra cost, and there is also a choice of either square back or rounded and backed.

To round off the whole operation Wheatons extend the advantages of

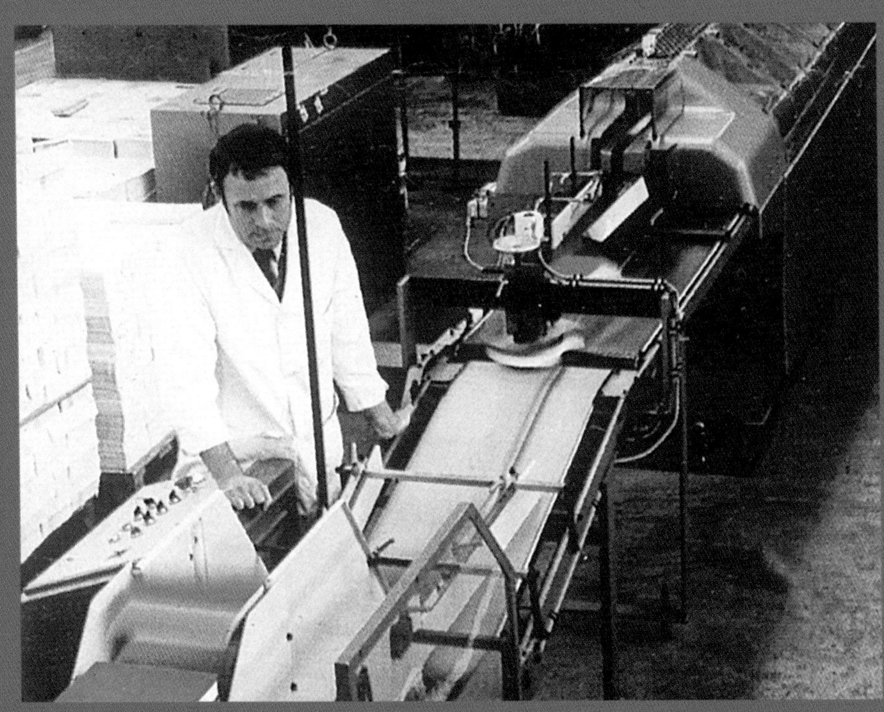

Tony Ellis overseeing the Kolbus Flowline

mass throughput to mailing. Addresses for their own Group journals are stored on computer at the Pergamon Press's Oxford headquarters. The computer prints these out as labels when they are needed, they are stuck on to cards and inserted into transparent plastic envelopes which are then heat sealed and sorted. Journals going abroad are divided into zones, and collected every day by the Post Office for world-wide airmail dispatch from Heathrow at virtually surface mail rates.

This can represent an enormous saving of both time and money. With so many of the journals printed at Exeter having a scientific content a relatively very large proportion do go overseas.

Throughout the production process the emphasis is on speed and this is achieved by concentrating on the flow-line concept. Combined with this is the extensive back-up at every stage – Wheatons even have their own generators.

Success has meant that further expansion along the same lines is being planned for next year and Wheatons are aiming to be one of the leading technical setting houses in Europe.

Their success has been based on a progressive understanding of modern publishers' needs. To meet these they have almost doubled their workforce since moving to the Marsh Barton site and they have spent £1.5m on new equipment.

They are finding new business on the Continent and they see the EEC market expanding. In addition to a London sales office, they have a Dutch agent.

"We know precisely what publishers want because we are publishers ourselves," says executive deputy chairman Anthony Wheaton. "New technology is going to play an important role in increasing specialization and reducing the number of suppliers in our market. To keep up with this technical typesetting and equipment developments considerable financial backing is needed. Because we are part of a successful, large group we have the backing to take full advantage of advances in technology. And as there is considerable demand for scientific and technical setting, we plan to expand significantly in that field." ■

The full page (A3) advert that accompanied the four page article

Continued from page 68

In support of building non-Group production accounts with publishers, Wheatons operated a London sales office at various central addresses during the 1970s and 1990s.

The London Sales Manager, Con O'Rourke, with Mike Nicholls, Ted Webb and later Hugh Brendon, was often required to act as an urgent courier, conveying packages and liaising with foreign embassies.

1980s The publishing department was successfully re-established in Exeter. In addition to the publishing of educational books, the department ventured into audio visual publishing in video cassette form for the school market. The Religious and Moral Education Press imprint continued.

In 1984 a successful association with Devon County Council was formed to publish local interest books on a profit share basis. Devon Books went on to publish over 100 titles in colour hard case style, all work being designed and printed within the company.

By the late 1980s the publishing department employed 30 staff in editorial, design and sales. However, the education market in the UK was changing towards computer-based learning programmes in schools. Printed books were declining. As pressure on small publishers increased and government funding to schools was reduced, there were significant mergers among the larger educational publishers.

Publishing Director John Halsall had retired and Simon Goodenough was appointed Publishing Director.

The Devon Books committee launch Devon Books.
Left to right: *Simon Goodenough; Managing Director – Wheaton Publishers, Geoffrey Household; Manager Devon Books, Peter Hunt; Devon CC – historian and author, Alec Coulter; Devon CC, Alison Shute; County Librarian, unknown, Gerry Bolt; Westcountry Books, Chairman DCC; Anthony Wheaton, Deputy Chairman – A Wheaton & Co, John Risdon; Westcountry Books.*

The Publishing Department Management

Managing Director
Simon Goodenough

Managing Editor (RMEP)
Mary Mears

Local Authority Publications Editor (Berkshire Books, Devon Books, Cornwall Books, Hampshire Books, Lincolnshire Books, Somerset Books)
Simon Butler

Design and Production Manager
Andy Jones

Sales Manager
Drummond Johnston

Educational Video
Barry Sutcliffe

Finance
Stephen Bright

1981 A serious dispute arose with the typesetting department staff, threatening the future of the department's 80 employees. Negotiations to reduce the costs of working, following high wage increases nationally agreed with the trade unions, ran into difficulties. The issues were eventually resolved through reorganisation and revised employment terms.

The company may well have employed over 500 staff in 1981. There is one record of payroll number 524, a bindery journeyman, but no other records of staff numbers remain available.

1982 The publishing company's sales were £1,031,000 and there was a management profit of £200,000.

Joint Managing Director and Sales Director Michael Keenan left the company. His deputy, John Seccombe, later took over the sales role.

1982–1986 The ebullient Robert Maxwell acquired the near-bankrupt British Printing Corporation, the largest printing group in the UK. This followed a dawn raid in 1981 securing a 29% stake and gaining full control in 1982. The price paid per share was just 25p or less. Maxwell changed the name to the British Printing and Communications Corporation (BPCC).

This major acquisition of BPCC marked a turning point as Maxwell's business interests developed, through BPCC involvement, from Pergamon's scientific publishing into multi-media publishing and contract printing of newspaper supplements and magazines.

In 1984 Robert Maxwell went on to purchase major American companies including The Webb Company of St Paul, Providence Gravure, Macmillan Inc, Science Research Association and the Official Airline Guide. In July 1984 he purchased Mirror Group Newspapers.

Rationalising BPCC's vast spread of UK printing companies, many unprofitable, involved intense negotiations with print unions and time consuming disputes and left him little time for Pergamon's affairs. Pergamon Press was later merged into BPCC.

On one occasion when Maxwell was engrossed in a union dispute at Odham Sun Watford, he ordered six of Wheatons FOCs up to his London office to meet him there to finalise another agreement. The FOCs returned to Exeter to report back to their colleagues and commented 'Maxwell is going through BPCC like the Red Army and we are not going to let it happen here'.

By 1986 the combined turnover of the BPCC UK and North American companies was £461.7 million employing 14,400 staff at 27 UK companies and 15 in the USA.

Continued on page 84

Wheaton's plan to win longer run business with a Super 70.

Polychrome has placed the first Rachwal 70 in Europe with Wheaton's in Exeter which intends to use the system to move into the directory market. Paul Simpson talks to Anthony Wheaton and Frank Wright.

This week Wheaton's will begin installing the first Rachwal Super 70 projection plate-making system in Europe. Wheaton's £250,000 investment in the Super 70 will be accompanied by a fourth coldset web, the Harris N420D, scheduled to arrive in October.

For Polychrome, which placed the Super 70 with Wheatons the order is a major coup. Another order for the 70 has already been placed by a large book firm.

Tom Heckles, managing director of Polychrome, confidently predicts that four Super 70 systems will be installed in the UK by the end on 1985.

Pergamon merger

Wheatons, a subsidiary of Pergamon Press was one of the first companies to buy the Opticopy 30/40 in 1981. The Opticopy will continue to be used for some of the scientific and technical publications. The idea behind the Rachwal Super 70 is to move the company into new markets.

A Wheaton & Co was founded in 1830 by William Wheaton which published the Alfred Wheaton Exeter Almanack. In 1906 the company began printing with a second-hand Columbian press.

Wheaton's became a well-known educational publisher and, in the 1950s began to take on and increasing amount of work for other publishers.

In 1966, Wheaton's merged with Pergamon Press. Two years later, on May 1968, a new bindery was opened. By November 1973 the company had moved completely to the site of its new bindery.

12 July 1985. The cover of LithoWeek *in which this article appeared*

Two factors seem to be characteristic of Wheaton's development: the continuation of the family link and the willingness for the company to leave old declining markets for newer, more promising fields.

Today Wheaton's prints 200 scientific and technical journals, from bi-monthlies to quarterlies. Most of the journal work is supplied by Pergamon.

The company also prints hard-cased books, including the Pergamon Leaders Of The World series, at Exeter. The publishing business has survived and last year the company set up a joint publishing venture with Devon County Council.

With 370 employees, including staff on the editorial side of the publishing company, and a turnover of £7 million in the current year, Wheaton's is one of Pergmon's most profitable subsidiaries.

Left to right: *Frank Wright, Anthony Wheaton, Michael Pegg of BPCC with Tom Heckles*

High Tech

The installation of the Super 70, which should be up and running by the autumn, is expected to increase the company's pre-press capacity for text and line work by 50 per cent.

The Super 70 plate making projection system has had a long gestation period. In 1977, at DRUPA, Rachwal unveiled a prototype of a 35m version of the Super 70.

Frank Wright, joint managing director at Wheatons, saw the system at DRUPA and was so impressed he decided to stay overnight to examine the product in greater detail.

By the time IPEX 1980 was held, Polychrome was able to show a

Trade Magazine Article

Wheatons' has been following the Super 70 since 1977

prototype of the 70mm model. In 1984, at IPEX, the 70mm high resolution system was given its full European launch.

Only a month or so before IPEX, Polychrome has been appointed as distributor for the whole range of Rachwal products in Europe.

The Super 70 was one of several new products Polychrome launched the Ipex, including the Co-Racer preview scanner. Most of the new products were hi-tech. 'We opened up the box and showed the world a hi-tech range of products' says Tom Heckels.

Before the last Ipex Polychrome had been seen largely as a traditional supplier of plates, films and inks. Tom Heckels sees the move onto hi-tech as a logical step, by simply offering a broader range of products to its existing markets

'We have always been strong in supplying plates to the book printing markets', says Tom Heckels. Polychrome had been supplying Wheaton's with plates since 1970.

Frank Wright says Wheaton's had followed the progress of the Super 70 since it first appeared in 1977. 'They were pushing us', says Tom Heckels, asking us what we were offering in that area.'

In fact Polychrome was supplying plates for the Dainippon Screen SAAPP system. Polychrome had a marketing agreement, enabling it to sell the SAAPP system, with its plates. The SAAPP system has now been installed at Biddles, Clays and Collins.

Frank Wright says that Wheaton's preferred to wait for the 70mm model. Polychrome developed the high resolution UV plates for the Rachwal Super 70 after being convinced of the potential of a 70mm system.

Anyone with any doubts about the market response to a 70mm projection plate making system only had to look at Rachwal's success in North America. Over 50 systems have been installed in the United States in the first two years of its existence.

Two of the most prominent installations are the California State printing plant in Sacramento and the Lawyers Corp in New York.

The Super 70 came on stream in Sacramento in August 1984 and Donald E Male, California State printer, says the system paid for itself in fifteen months. 'one of the advantages', says Tom Heckels, 'is that the Super 70 stats paying for itself from day one, by saving film'.

Officials at the Office of State Printing in Sacramento saw the Super 70m version at a graphics arts show in San Francisco. Donald E Male says that the Super 70 was a step in the right direction but he preferred to wait for a system that could expose eight pages up.

A year later, Mr Males saw the Rachwal's camera system which could be linked to the Super 70 and used with the state printing plant's typesetting system.

Using the camera mounted on the photo-composition unit, the OSP eliminated RC paper, replacing it with an image recorded on 70 mm film, enabling the printer to go straight from photo-composition to the projection plate-maker.

Mr Male estimates that annual savings are around $300,000. The system is used to print changes in legislation, regulations and reports of meetings where such changes are discussed.

Technicians at the Californian state printing plant are talking about interspersing half tones with the line work but that is very much in the future.

The Super 70 system at the Lawyers Corp is being used for similar work. Lawyers Corp send notices of changes in state and Federal legislation to lawyers subscribing to the service.

Mr Heckels believes the 35mm version was basically suitable for 'mass market paperbacks'.

In May, the Polychrome Corporation injected a 'substantial amount of investment capital', into Rachal. 'It is an arms length investment', says Tom Heckels. 'We are not involved in the day to day running of the company, though our R & D teams are working together on new developments'.

Rachwal succeeded in developing the Super 70 because it concentrated exclusively on breaking through the 35mm barrier. 'They specialize entirely in projection systems', says Tom Heckels.

The Super 70 plate-making system has three basic elements: camera station, control console and projection plate-maker. The Super 70 uses an advanced micro optical storage technique (MOST) to photograph and store camera ready copy on high resolution 70mm film. The camera station can capture up to 500 A4 pages on a roll at ten seconds a page.

With speeds like that, throughput is obviously the major selling point. Wheaton's plans to continue using Opticopy on some technical journals because of the variable quality of the artwork supplied by contributors. The system works best when camera ready copy is of uniform standard.

The heart of the Super 70 is a computer console which determines all plate-making functions. Image positioning, plate exposure and imposition layout are controlled from the VDU work station. Job layouts for trim, margins and plate sizes can be changed to suit the work load. The imposition system also has a large colour screen.

Polychrome supplies PPN grain anodized negative plates, which are exposed in the projection plate-maker, every five seconds. The 147 x 194 complete area enable two plates to be mounted simultaneously in the plate-maker. Wheaton's already uses PPN 6 plates.

To take the process one step further Rachwal launched the photo-composer camera in the US which takes pages off a photo-composer's CRT, straight through to plate-maker. The California State printing plant uses its camera to take pages off a Volt auto-logic APS System.

Tom Heckels says the camera is available in the UK for interfacing with a Triple-I system, a Hell Digiset or an APS 5. Polychromatic hopes to link the camera to the Monotype Lasercomp in the near future.

The major saving with the Super 70 system is film. Rachwal claims that the

Super 70 will save up to 90 per cent of a company's film costs.

The second major saving is time: the 70 is best suited to fast throughput publications and parts catalogues. RBW Press in Montreal has intended to use the Super 70 for directories but has been swamped with demand for parts catalogues from the motor industry in Detroit.

Wheaton's has built up a reputation as a short run press specialist, but with the Super 70, Anthony Wheaton, executive deputy chairman, sees the company moving into longer run work.

'The expansion we see with the Rachwal will be in the field of directories, encyclopaedias, technical books, catalogues and lists'.

'The jobs will be 500 to 1000 pages with runs of 10,000–20,000. We are predominately talking text and line work, says Anthony Wheaton.

This new business will replace some of the fall off in educational sales. 'Educational publishing has been severely affected by the recession', says Anthony Wheaton. We had to look for new markets'.

Run lengths for scientific and technical journals printed at Wheaton's used to average about 2,500. Today that figure has dropped to nearer 1,000.

Faced with such a drop in print runs, Wheaton's work force has had to become skilled in the art of fast make ready.

'We can make ready in six or seven minutes', says Anthony Wheaton. 'The idea is to treat each new title a though it is just another section'. Between 20 and 30 titles pass through the press room each day of the week and Frank Wright says 'We have to be slick with that quantity.'

> Wheaton: 'I was in my garden sweeping up the leaves on a Saturday afternoon when Robert Maxwell phoned with instructions for us to typeset the *Radio Times*.'

Wheaton's uses several techniques to ensure that each new title can be swiftly put on the press. Anthony Wheaton says the tree essential ingredients are: batch production, standardization of format and standardization of paper. How these factors will be affected if Wheaton's picks up a lot of directory business, remains to be seen.

Last year Wheaton's bought a Muller Martini Normbinder to back up its existing monobloc line, and a capacity to bind some 200,000 flexibacks a week, as well as some hard case books.

The next round will probably be in typesetting. Just as Wheaton's has evolved its own way of working in the press room, the company has adapted its two Bedford front end systems for mathematical setting.

Wheaton's has 25 input terminals and five input correction terminals, with the possibility of page make-up, if the department were not so busy. The front end system is driving two Monotype Laser-comps.

'We have designed our own keyboard for setting display symbols in mathematics', says Anthony Wheaton. Special symbols are often required for

Wheatons' designed its own mathematics keyboard and also handled the printing of Deng Xiao Ping's collected speeches and writings.

the technical journals that Wheaton's specializes in printing and setting.

Although most of the technical journals are monthlies, bi-monthlies and quarterlies, the company also recently had to cope with one of Britain's largest weekly tiles, the *Radio Times.*

After the closure of BPCC's Park Royal plant in November 1983, Robert Maxwell had to find another company to set the *Radio Times*.

'I was working in my garden one Saturday afternoon', recalls Anthony Wheaton, 'When our group chairman Robert Maxwell telephoned me with instructions for our plant to take over the typesetting of the next issue of the *Radio Times*'.

As it turned out, the Radio Times was set at Wheaton's for almost eighteen months. In early 1985, BPCC began to reduce the amount of text set at Wheaton's passing some of the work to BPCC's new London typesetting centre.

Now that the typesetting centre is fully on stream, Wheaton's has stopped setting the *Radio Times* and both it and *The Listener* are now set in London.

Handling that amount of work, up to 1500 pages a week, at such short notice, is a feat that Anthony Wheaton is rather proud of. Wheaton's is not in fact, a member of BPCC.

The original investment will probably be to give Wheaton's substantial data base facilities. 'We expect to find an increasing demand in future to take text from authors and publishers in a machine readable form', says Anthony Wheaton.

To help the company exploit that market, Anthony Wheaton recently negotiated an agreement with the NGA, allowing the company to take text from floppy disks.

Being the first to install a piece of kit like the Super 70 can have its drawbacks. There are too many companies which have splashed out on the new technology and seen profits cut back as the management struggle to get to grips with the new machine.

Still Frank Wright, and the printing manager, Kenny Baker are confident they should be able to cope with the problems. Frank Wright has already pinpointed several problem areas, such as the positioning of camera ready copy, where he wants to eliminate 'eye balling'.

'There are usually problems' he says. 'But we have always managed to cope with them in the past'. ■

Continued from page 77

1976–1985 Wheatons were innovative in developing cutting edge production facilities relevant to the needs of scientific, academic and general publishers, particularly for short run publications.

These plant investments required considerable change in working practices at Wheatons and involved lengthy, but eventually successful, negotiations with print unions and company union chapels.

By the mid-1970s, and to provide for further evolution in the way author text would be handled, without compositors keying from traditional manuscript copy, the company negotiated with the National Graphical Association union (NGA) the first UK 'new sources' agreement. This agreement provided for text to be received as camera-ready copy (CRC) to be used directly for plate making without the need to re-typeset, or in machine readable form as Telecoms line data, magnetic tape, compact disc, by aerial or any other future means.

The agreement broke new ground in avoiding previous restrictive practices and took two years to negotiate.

At that time the internet was in the very early stages of development in the USA and not yet available worldwide.

The 3M Pyrofax system 1976. Transferring camera copy pages direct to printing plates using electronically charged fuser technology

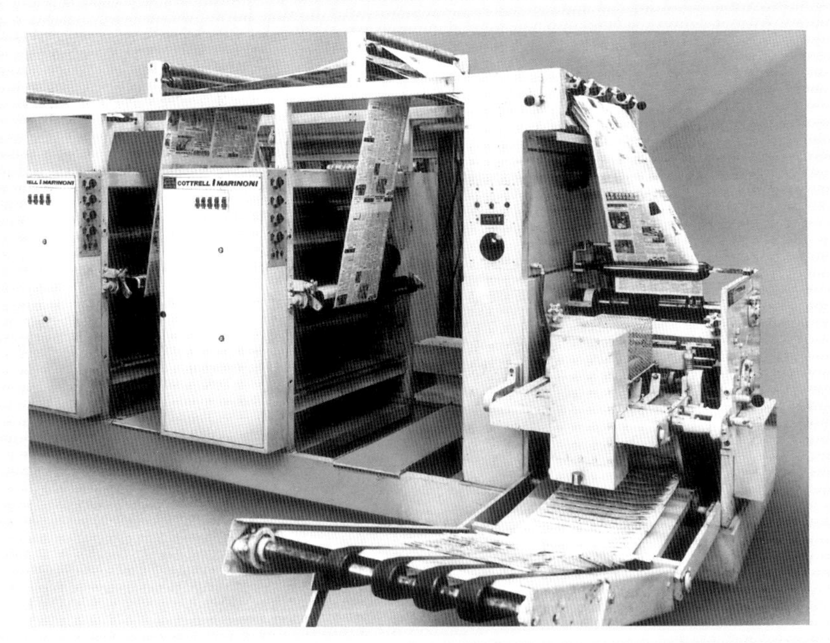

1970s to 1980s Cotterell Marinoni cold-set web offset presses – models N420B (above) and N429D (top right) three Cotterell Marinoni's were installed in the company.

Industry firsts were:

1972 Wheatons was one of the first UK book printers to use Cottrell Marinoni and Harris mini-web offset presses for short run work of typically 1,000 to 3,000 copies.

1976 3M Pyrofax, a low cost plate-making system used for camera-ready text direct to printing plate without the need for film.

1980 Opticopy – a page-imposing camera system prior to litho plate making, used for higher quality text and illustrations.

1972 –1980 Development of US-made Bedford Computers' financial typesetting system to set complex mathematical text in realtime display on computer screens without prior encoding input, using 30 multi-shift keyboards with layouts designed by Wheatons' staff addressing all mathematical symbols and characters. Output was to two Monotype Lasercomp film setters.

1978 First installation in Europe of US-made Rachwal Super 70 page-imposing graphic plate-making system operating at 10 seconds per page and saving 90% of prior film costs.

Wheatons were the first in Exeter to install a word processor for office use – the US Wang system.

The Rachwal Super 70 system from 1978. The camera station photographing camera-ready pages to 70mm roll film. The computer controlled imaging unit then enlarged the pages to reproduction size stepping each page to the printing plate.

1984 Wheatons, including publishing and retail, now employed over 450 staff and was one of the few large industrial employers in Exeter.

1984: *Directors of South West Publishing and Arts, the publishers of Regional Magazines*
Left to right: *Jane Jones, Anthony Wheaton and Mark Jones.*

Wheatons were awarded Robert Maxwell's personal award for productivity improvement in a Group company.

In January a controlling interest was acquired in Exeter-based magazine publisher Regional Magazines Ltd. This company published A4 format monthly local interest magazines in colour. Titles were *Devon Life* and five other county titles in the South West. All were printed at Wheatons.

Pergamon Press was one of the early UK companies to open an office in Bejing, China. A Chinese publishing trade delegation was invited to the UK by Pergamon and visited Wheatons. To celebrate the visit the company printed an edition in English of the speeches of Deng Xaoping, Chairman of the Chinese Communist Party at the time.

More skilled print workers were required than could be recruited locally. The company was able to arrange with Exeter City Council for an allocation of council houses to help to recruit key workers.

The 'Pergamon Electronic Resource' commenced. The objective of this venture between Pergamon, Wheatons and Pergamon Graphics (Derby) was to develop in phases a Group database publishing facility based on the Unix operating system from Bell Laboratories in the USA. The objective was to store on computer in searchable form Pergamon's major reference works which were computer typeset at Wheatons, with a view to enabling researchers, academics and professionals to abstract individual articles or papers online rather than purchasing complete printed copies.

American database development consultants, Burrell Associates Washington, who had completed a similar project for a large American publisher, were brought in to advise and accelerate the work.

Being before the advent of the internet, the project proved to be ahead of its time and after two years it was shelved.

The Electronic Resource continued, however, in providing online Pergamon's growing list of electronic journals and liaising with Pergamon Infoline, London.

1984: *Chinese publishing delegation's visit to Pergamon Press and Wheatons with Anthony Wheaton, Frank Wright and Sara Warren PA.*

A.WHEATON & CO.LTD
A. WHEATON & CO
RECEPTION

Staff Presentations

1981 Commemorating Keith Richard's (litho printer) 25 years' service with the company **Left to right:** *Ken Baker, Keith Richards, Anthony Wheaton, Mr and Mrs Mike Hawker*

1984 Left to right: *Edward Boobier, Bob Mitchell, Anthony Wheaton, E Burt, Andy Williams*

1984
Sports and Social Club

Left to right: Ken Skinner, David Lee, Keith Napper. The others are visitors to the club

A Good Side

Pete Webber, Journals Production Manager, recalls an occasion when Robert Maxwell toured the factory:

'I was in the Offprints Department of the Bindery chatting with Bob Edwards whilst Maureen Appleton, Debbie Hughes, and two others, including Joyce Connet, were stood at the work bench making-up offprints. Mr Maxwell and his entourage entered through the Despatch Department which was nearby. He stopped for a quick chat, noticed the girls were standing for hours to make-up offprints and that Joyce Connett was quite elderly. Maxwell instructed Bob Edwards to go to the Schools Department, run by Barbara Marchant, and obtain a high-stool for Joyce to sit on. He stayed chatting with us until Bob returned.

I know Mr Maxwell received some bad press but he also had a good side'.

The Countries of the World Information and Leaders of the World series

From 1970 to 1990 Pergamon published two major series of reference publications.

Robert Maxwell's understanding of the complex and volatile political situation in Eastern Europe in the 1980s and at the time of the ending of the Cold War was arguably unique for a Western publisher.

Arising from his experiences in Berlin at the end of World War II and speaking fluent Russian, Czech and German, he was able to develop top level contacts with the leaders of the Eastern bloc countries and the scientific community. His reputation with the authorities within the Soviet Union countries bordering the West became such that he could obtain audiences with presidents and heads of state with relative ease.

A series of major publications followed giving historical and statistical information on Eastern bloc countries for the Western observer, researcher and businessman.

Events were followed by the peoples' uprising, the fall of the Berlin wall and the reunification of Germany.

The following publications were launched during these years all of which were printed by Wheatons:

- *Information GDR*
- *Information Bulgaria*
- *Information Czechoslovakia*
- *Information Poland*
- *Information Estonia*
- *Information Romania*

Later –

- *Information China*
- *Information Mongolia*

Under the World Leaders biographical series the following titles were published:

- *Brezhnev*
- *Kurt Waldheim*

1983–5 Following labour disputes at BPCC Watford printing plants, Odhams and Sun Printers, the BPCC typesetting company at Park Royal London was to be closed in November 1983. The £20 million printing contract with the BBC for the *Radio Times* and the *Listener* were at immediate risk.

Robert Maxwell called upon Wheatons to take over the typesetting with immediate effect and until a new planned London Typesetting Centre was available. In the event this was to happen nearly 18 months later. There was no other Group company which could aspire to the task.

An accommodation with the London NGA branch was agreed enabling Wheatons' NGA members to handle the work but on the basis that some redundant London NGA typesetters who were familiar with the *Radio Times*, would be re-engaged in Exeter on a temporary basis. Arrangements were successfully made with Wheatons' staff to forgo all holidays and Saturdays and to work longer shift hours to create the necessary capacity.

Left: *Russian delegation executives in the bindery examining work in progress with Mike Keenan and Anthony Wheaton*

A BBC editorial team, including Editor Brian Gearing at times was accommodated in Exeter hotels and two A3 format fax machines were installed on dedicated telephone lines to the BBC.

The 1983 Christmas double issue of the *Radio Times* was completed and delivered on time to meet press deadlines at five UK printing plants printing a total of 10.026 million copies, and selling into one in six households in the UK.

When it became clear that the exercise would have to be extended for many months, a second Bedford typesetting system was imported from the USA to increase capacity and dependability.

The work progressively built up to 17 weekly regional editions of the *Radio Times* totalling 1,500 pages per week delivered to UK printing plants on Wednesday nights by air charter from Exeter Airport. With union unrest continuing amongst BPCC Watford printing plants at this time, tension was high and there was always a risk of flying pickets.

Throughout the period until early 1985 the extra work was in addition to the underlying Pergamon journal typesetting programme. By Easter 1985 the *Radio Times* was transferred in stages to the newly operating BPCC London Typesetting Centre. However, the higher wage rates and bonuses paid during the *Radio Times* period proved hard to bring back in line, ultimately leading to disputes.

1985 By now British book production companies were experiencing a downturn in their markets. Printers' prices to publishers could not keep pace with increases in costs – mostly wages boosted during the years of high UK inflation.

Overseas printers in the Far East and Europe were by now 10 to 15% more competitive. By 1986 26% of UK book production work, particularly colour, was being placed overseas and the trend was increasing.

Wheatons lost their largest non-Group customer, Macmillan Publishers, based at Basingstoke, who had set up a production office in Hong Kong with eight UK staff and transferred their printing work to Hong Kong and China. Economies had to be made at Exeter. Cost saving measures and 18 redundancies were eventually agreed with unions.

With his attention now turned to resolving BPCC's affairs and with further acquisitions to come, Robert Maxwell never visited Wheatons again.

Union Recognition

From the 1950s to the mid-1980s, Wheatons was a member of the Master Printers Association which later became the British Printing Industries Federation (BPIF) and recognised the print trade unions. The BPIF undertook, on behalf of its members, the annual wage and conditions of employment negotiations with the print unions' negotiating panels at national level.

The outcome of these negotiations, subject to members' ratification, formed the basis of wage rate reviews at company level including overtime rates, shift premiums, machine extras, holiday pay, etc.

In the mid-1980s Robert Maxwell cancelled BPIF membership for Wheatons and the other Pergamon Print Division companies in the UK to save the not unsubstantial subscription costs which were based on payroll numbers. This was on the basis that negotiations would thereafter be conducted at company level but taking into account the terms agreed at national level between the BPIF and the unions. However, this annual practice became onerous and time consuming for management and incurred lost production time by key print workers who were allowed time off for union duties on full pay. A settlement with one chapel (union representatives in one department) could lead to a counter claim from another.

From the 1960s and into the 1980s and beyond, the print unions (along with their peers in UK manufacturing industries) were well organised, influential and naturally determined to hold on to previously agreed wage levels and rights on behalf of their membership.

When redundancies or major cost-saving measures were required, prior consultations with unions were necessary. Meetings with unions would often involve respective Branch Secretaries and if issues were not resolved, National Officers would later be called in. To organise such meetings could take months, and if issues were still not resolved and the meeting adjourned it could take months again to agree a new date. In the meantime, the status quo would be maintained. Management soon became familiar with an old union adage: 'new money once given shall not (easily) be taken away'.

Members of the following unions were employed by the company:

- The Typographical Association (TA) – typesetters – which later became the National Graphical Association (NGA)
- Amalgamated Society of Lithographic Printers (ASLP) – litho printers and plate makers
- National Society of Operative Printers and Assistants (NATSOPA) – printers' assistants
- Society of Graphical and Allied Trades (SOGAT) – bindery staff
- Society of Lithographic Artists Designers and Engravers (SLADE) – camera operators and graphic artists
- National Union of Journalists (NUJ) – editorial (in part).

Over the years the craft unions merged as did the non-craft unions. The union integrations were driven by the dramatic changes in the trade and the decline of the printing industry occasioned by technical change. All sections of commercial print, book printing, publishing and the media were affected, resulting in progressively declining union membership and influence.

By 2016 all of these unions had merged and integrated with the UNITE union representing the print industry as a whole. Wheatons had just two remaining chapels representing union members in the printing department and the bindery.

Working hours and shift patterns

Expensive main plant had to be operated over the optimum available hours for ultimate investment cost recovery and contribution to company overheads leading to profitable operation.

To achieve this objective, a balance of skilled staff and consistent work loading from chosen markets had to be built up and maintained.

The company working patterns were based on day work hours in office staff departments. The working week was initially 40 hours and later 37½ hours. Overtime in factory departments was paid on the basis of the first four hours on Saturdays at time and a half, then double time, and double time on Sundays.

As the company developed in the 1960s shift work was introduced on principal production plant. From the 1970s shift work became more widespread.

The following shift patterns applied in factory departments:

- Double day shift 6 a.m. to 2 p.m. and 2 p.m. to 10 p.m. with 20 minute breaks on each shift and a ten minute overlap for briefing the next shift
- By the 1980s a three-shift pattern was introduced on key plant to provide 24-hour working. Triple shift involved working 6 a.m. to 2 p.m. and 2 p.m. to 10 p.m. and 10 p.m. to 6 a.m. Mondays to Thursdays. On Fridays hours were 6 a.m. to 11.30 a.m. and 11.30 a.m. to 5 p.m. and 5 p.m. to 10.30 p.m.

Shift working carried a plus 20% pay premium over day work rates.

- By 2016 a system of quasi-shifts was part introduced when more flexibility of working hours was required at times. This involved working 6 a.m. to 1.30 p.m. and 10.30 p.m. to 6 a.m. at a 10% pay premium.

BANK OF ENGLAND
I Promise to pay the Bearer on Demand the Sum of
B09 941813
Five Pounds
BANK of ENGLAND
I Promise to pay the Bearer on Demand the sum of
One Pound
Elizabeth R
57S 235128
57S 235129
57S 235130
57S 2351
BANK OF ENGLAND
I promise to pay the Bearer on Demand the sum of
M75 324153
Ten shillings
10 SHILLINGS
10 SHILLINGS
LONDON
For the Gov. and Compa. of the
BANK of ENGLAND
J. S. Fforde.
Chief Cashier
M75 324153

The Production Bonus Scheme

From the early 1960s, Wheatons operated a production bonus scheme in factory departments.

The Personnel Administration (PA) bonus scheme was based on work study to set production values for every individual stage of the production processes, particularly in typesetting and in the bindery. Printing and the bindery operations were mostly 'machine controlled' and bonuses were calculated on a more average basis provided that rated machine speeds were maintained.

The PA scheme was adopted by many of the UK book printing companies at the time and by some newspapers. In 1960 Anthony Wheaton was sent for bonus scheme initiation training with the PA consultant at the Brighton Argus newspaper for 6 months. He worked there as a studyman on the team setting up a scheme for the Linotype operators.

The basis of the scheme was to set a standard value for a brisk but sustainable rate of working, including allowance for breaks throughout the working day or shift. This pace of working was rated as a 133 performance and was the starting point for production bonuses paid in addition to basic pay levels. For work performance assessed as above this level an additional bonus was available on a scale up to a top limit and cut off at a 167 performance.

Having completed purpose designed daily worksheets recording the time taken for each operation, personal performances were calculated against the set values for the operations. This work was undertaken by the Work Study Department and assessors headed by Ken Skinner.

The scheme relied on keeping work values up to date and having all elements covered. Setting the values involved 'studymen' with stop watches recording time taken for elements of work against their judgement of the performance (pace of working) of the employee at the time, applied to the rating scale, i.e.133, 140, 150, etc. Back at the Work Study Office this information would enable the setting of the values. There were no calculators at the time – slide rules and Contex adding machines were used.

If work practices changed through the introduction of new equipment or more productive hand work routines, etc. the values would need to be updated (re-studied) to avoid the values becoming slack. Slack values led to over payment of bonus.

Initially, the bonus calculator was linked to pay and was adjusted annually in line with wage increases. The link was unshackled in 1968 and thereafter the value of bonus payment remained unchanged annually.

The scheme ran for 23 years until it became outdated and costly to maintain. The scheme was phased out and replaced by negotiated house merit money payments by 1986 and the Work Study Department was disbanded.

Plaque

This plaque hung in Wheatons' Boardroom from the 1960s until the 1990s. It was read by visiting national union officers – often with an acknowledgement but no comment!

The text was hand typeset from cased metal type by compositor Len Coleman, in about 1964, shortly before his retirement.

At the time, Wheatons still had one compositor who took snuff from his forearm, a printer's tradition from Victorian times, designed to avoid lead poisoning.

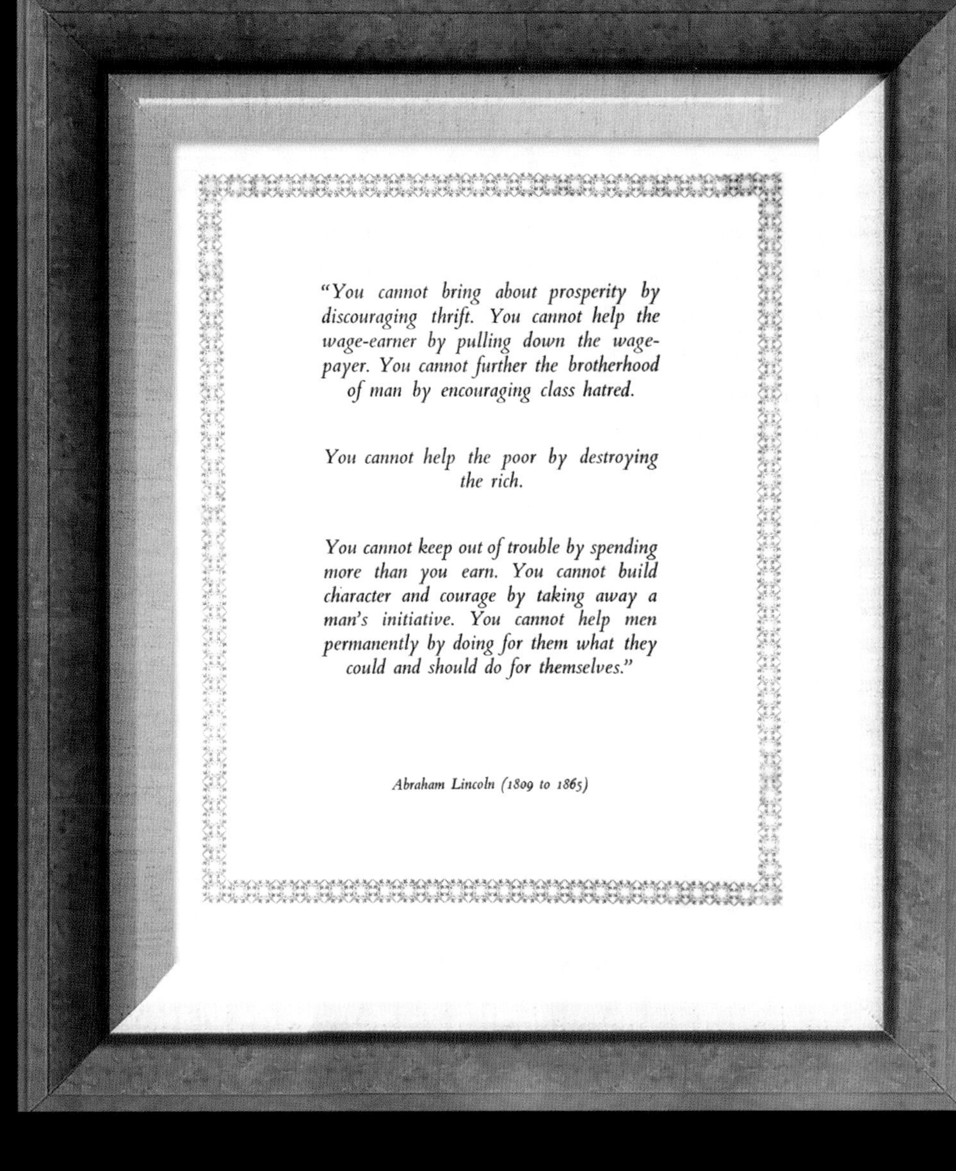

"You cannot bring about prosperity by discouraging thrift. You cannot help the wage-earner by pulling down the wage-payer. You cannot further the brotherhood of man by encouraging class hatred.

You cannot help the poor by destroying the rich.

You cannot keep out of trouble by spending more than you earn. You cannot build character and courage by taking away a man's initiative. You cannot help men permanently by doing for them what they could and should do for themselves."

Abraham Lincoln (1809 to 1865)

1986: *Brochures of the BPCC Book Group*

The BPCC Era

In April 1986, Wheatons was transferred from Pergamon Press ownership to the British Printing and Communications Corporation (BPCC) and joined the recently formed Book Group with a combined turnover of £34 million.

The Book Group comprised:

- **Dorstel Press Ltd,** Harlow
- **Hazell Watson & Viney Ltd,** Aylesbury
- **Purnell Book Production Ltd,** Paulton
- **A Wheaton & Co Ltd,** Exeter.

Anthony Wheaton was appointed Marketing Director of the Book Group in addition to remaining Deputy Chairman of Wheatons, EPC Dublin and Aberdeen University Press. Also continuing was liaison with Pergamon on technical typesetting and data-base developments.

The BPCC directors without, as yet, much experience of working with Robert Maxwell and mindful of Anthony Wheaton's Pergamon Press background, wanted to ensure their own managerial influence at Wheatons and appointed their own Managing Director, Jim Myers, in 1986.

Maxwell acquired a controlling interest in the British Printing Corporation in 1981. Later, with a view to developing into communications as well as print, he added a C to form BPCC. The various directors of the Book Group were appointed from Group companies (only one from the main board) and they had limited experience of working with Maxwell.

Liaison between the Book Group companies was through monthly board meetings chaired by Group Chief Executive Michael Pegge. The meetings would be held at each company on rotation and include factory update visits.

The UK book production industry was continuing to face severe competition from overseas, and UK printers were competing with each other for remaining work at low prices. A progressive contraction of the industry followed, with many well known and established companies closing. This was a trend that was to continue through the next 15 years.

By October 1986 operating costs had to be reduced whilst retaining key skills. The outcome of a root and branch review of Wheatons' administrative and middle management was announced. Measures were taken to tighten up and integrate some administrative sections and reorganise management roles.

Fifteen staff redundancies were announced, together with 8 changes in managers' responsibilities. Also, the work performance related incentive bonus scheme (see page 97) in factory departments was becoming obsolete due to changing working practices. The scheme was phased out after operating for some 23 years.

Later, the company now with 380 staff and sales of £7,783,000 was divided into separate operating units:

- BPCC Wheatons Ltd – book printing and binding
- BPCC Techset Ltd – scientific typesetting
- Oyez Wheatons Ltd – commercial stationers
- Wheaton Publishers Ltd – publishing

The Book Group refocused sales objectives with each company specialising more closely in their selected markets.

BPCC Techset, which took over the 85 staff of the Composing Room (typesetting department), was set up to respond to the changing market requirements in technical typesetting from Wheatons' main customers.

The Bedford real time text and mathematic typesetting system was upgraded to a Bedford Target Vision Network System with 27 text input terminals and ten intelligent editing terminals. The output typesetters were upgraded to a Monotype Lasercomp Mark II and a Monotype Lasercomp Pioneer to output text with graphics to film pages.

By 1998 to1999 the way scientific publishers were presenting their work for printing was changing (as was anticipated when previously negotiating the 'new sources' agreement). Some conventional typesetting from manuscript copy continued for complex work involving mathematics symbols. However the increasing requirement was for text work to be received directly from technical authors who had prepared their research papers as computer files on disc from PCs. Pergamon, and later Elsevier, were increasingly supplying finished journal and academic book pages as complete computer files ready for imposition and output, direct to printing plates. In addition, pages were also presented as hard copy (camera-ready copy or CRC) finished pages.

Techset was accommodated within the factory in premises previously occupied by the Sports & Social Club. The Social Club relocated to premises at Clifton Hill, Exeter, organised by the club's enthusiastic secretary, Peter Webber.

Wheatons' commercial stationery business was located within the factory complex adjacent to the bindery and served the Marsh Barton business community and school customers. It was sold in December 1986 to Oyez Stationers of London which had national branches.

Wheaton Publishers Ltd continued, largely independently and unaffected by the reorganisation. BPCC were printers and under their ownership there was effectively no publishing senior management experience or directional involvement with the company.

The Publishing Department had a creative graphic studio headed by Andy Jones. Their work involved book illustration, conceptual layout and design, cover designs and artwork. The studio had evolved from the Art Department at Fore Street in the 1950s headed by Lloyd Petherick which employed commercial artists. They were the cartographers for the atlases and commercial artists. Wheatons undertook work for Great Western Railway. Lloyd Petherick produced artwork for the well-known railway posters printed by Wheatons,

1984 Wheaton Publishers Ltd: *One of the graphic designers, Maggie Ginger and editor Simon Butler, discuss promotional designs for the Wheaton Publishers Catalogue – Simon Butler went on to become an Editorial Director of Wheaton Publishers Ltd.*

This photograph of the design studio was taken before its introduction to state-of-the-art Apple Mac technology.

displayed at stations and on trains advertising places such as Torbay and the English Riviera as tourist destinations after the war.

1987 As Robert Maxwell's overall interests shifted further towards media publishing and watchful of Rupert Murdoch's News Corps' international expansion, he renamed BPCC Maxwell Communications Corporation (MCC).

He announced the objective of 'becoming a global information and communications company before the end of the decade with annual revenues of £3–5 billion with earnings to match'.

1988/89 As the UK book production industry declined further, MCC announced that it was splitting the Book Group into the BPCC Journals & Reference Book Division (including Wheatons) and BPCC Books Ltd and was to concentrate its main business on more profitable commercial print, contract newspaper supplements and national magazine production contracts. By 1990 BPCC Books Ltd was disbanded. Purnell Book Production, Dorstel Press and Hazell, Watson and Viney Ltd were run down and closed.

The exception was Wheatons which was still trading profitably, operating mainly in the more specialised academic markets and commercial publications. The Book Plan service to general publishers continued. The programme of Pergamon journals was key to the future of the ongoing business.

A typical range of book and journal production produced by the company

Roland 800 printing press, sheet size 1,000 x 1,400 mm – printing colour books and magazines

Regional Magazines, publishers of a stable of A4 colour county magazines, with Managing Editor Mark Jones and a staff of some 30 editors, advertisement sales and administrative staff, moved from Southernhay into the ex-Wheatons' publishing offices at Marsh Barton. This publisher was later sold to a media company.

The rapid expansion by acquisition of BPCC and now MCC from 1984 to 1988 was largely financed by term bank loans to be repaid from expected improved earnings and increased sales and from rationalisation within the Group. The high level of borrowings over the relatively short period was to prove an insurmountable burden.

In 1988, after two years as Book Group Marketing Director, Anthony Wheaton was offered the role of Group Sales Director based in London.

One of the Regional Magazine publications

With a detailed knowledge of the shrinking book market and anticipating the difficulties which the Book Group Companies would experience, he declined and left BPCC.

1989 Under increasing pressure from banks and financial institutions to repay due loans, Robert Maxwell was forced to sell Pergamon's 'crown jewels' — the scientific journals, to Reed Elsevier in Holland. The price was £440 million. A contract was signed enabling Wheatons to continue producing the journals.

Also sold to raise further funds was a 49% stake in the Mirror Group.

1990 In May Jim Myers resigned as Managing Director. Previous Book Group Finance Director David Beatty was appointed Managing Director at Wheatons. Also in May, Angus Clark joined the company as Director and General Manager with Group Chief Executive Michael Pegge closely involved.

1991 Publishing continued until eventually it became unprofitable and, no longer being part of Wheatons' core activity, Wheaton Publishers Ltd was closed in 1991 with the loss of 31 employees.

Between 1980 and1992 a number of successful local businesses were started by experienced ex-Wheaton staff:

- Devon Books imprint was sold and continued as a part of Halsgrove Publishers, Wellington.
- RMEP (Religious and Moral Education Press), an imprint of Wheaton Publishers, was sold to Hymns Ancient and Modern, Norwich. Publications continued to be commissioned and edited by Mary Mears, the ex-Editorial Manager of Wheatons. She was then employed by Hymns Ancient and Modern and worked from her Newton Abbot Office.
- Andy Jones, the publishing department's Design and Production Manager and Barry Sutcliffe the Educational Video Production Manager set up Topics – The Creative Partnership, a book packagers, providing publishing services (including book design and project management) for the publishing industry.
- Drummond Johnstone, the Publishing Sales Manager, set up Southgate Publishers and Mosaic Educational – publishers of educational materials.
- Ex-print department employees, Andy Gliddon and Murray Couch set up their own print business, Short Run Press Ltd, Exeter – book and journal printers.
- Colin Tucker set up Monospools Typesetting which became Exe Valley Design and Print.
- Tom Gorfin set up Vine & Gorfin in Exmouth.
- Chris Woolacott, one of the platemaking staff, together with Ron Ward set up Peninsular Repro.
- Mike Cole, one of the managers in the typesetting department, set up P & M Typesetters Ltd.
- The print producton manager David Miller, set up Studio Publishing, in Dawlish.
- Wheaton Publisher's Editorial Director, Simon Butler became a founding shareholder in Halsgrove Publishing in Wellington.

1991 On 5 November Robert Maxwell was found drowned having apparently fallen from his motor yacht the *Lady Ghislaine*, off the Canary Islands in the most suspicious circumstances.

Maxwell's death triggered a flood of instability for MCC with banks frantically calling in their loans. It was a Swiss bank that blew the whistle tripping the collapse when it called in the Serious Fraud Office and put a receiver into Headington Investments (a Maxwell company) after discovering that the security the bank was owed against a loan had been sold. MCC struggled to remain in business and applied for bankruptcy protection in 1992.

Maxwell's sons Kevin and Ian, already in the business, did their best to keep MCC trading but lengthy litigation ensued over several years eventually leading to administrators being appointed.

Administrators Arthur Anderson were called in to try to salvage MCC (including BPCC) which was reported to be at least £1 billion in debt.

Arthur Anderson administration lasted for several years owing to the complex tangle of relationships it uncovered between the various companies.

The plight of the Maxwell pensioners made the national press. It came to light that £440 million had been withdrawn from the various Group pension schemes. The pension schemes (set up in 1985) were found to have a shortfall in funds of £276 million which took years to address.

1994 Angus Clark, a BPCC Divisional Director since 1992 and already with the company was appointed Managing Director of Wheatons also encompassing the BPCC Science and Information Division Companies.

1995 A 'global settlement' was secured by Lord John Cuckney, appointed by the Labour Government at the time, with members of the city institutions and banks caught up in the BPCC affairs. A £276 million settlement was arranged to reinstate the underfunded pension schemes. As part of the deal the government agreed to waive scheme liabilities of some £100 million of State Scheme Premiums (SSP).

However, the 'global settlement' was not applied ethically by the trustees across the various pension schemes. The BPCC staff scheme (including Pergamon Press staff) was left short by £30 million whereas other BPCC schemes received £30 million too much. The government took this money and set it against the SSP shortfall of £100 million.

A group Pension Plan Consultative Committee (about 2002 – 2007) was set up to meet government minister Frank Field, Chairman of the Select Committee, and Peter Lilley, Minister for

1992 Wheatons' Team Royal Marine assault course, Lympstone. **Left to right:** *Bob Brown, Phil Dale, Ron Ward (Peninsular Repro), Chris Sharrock and Peter Leach.*

1993 Wheatons Team BPCC Endurance Course at the Royal Marines training area Woodbury Common. **Left to right: *Top row***, *Peter Leach, Chris Sharrock, Bob Brown.* **Bottom row**: *Yvette Bartlett (nee Bellamy), Paul Cummings and Helen Carnell.*

1998 The BPCC Intergroup Event Royal Marine assault course, Woodbury Common. **Left to right:** *Iain Littlejohn; (BPCC Wheatons/WhiteFriars graduate trainee), Bob Brown, Chris Sharrock, David Bulfurd; (Whitefriars), Paul Cummings and Claire (Whitefriars).*

1995. *The Harris 2 unit A4 web press for book and journal printing. The press replaced one of the ageing Cotterell Marinoni presses.*

1995. *The Commercial department at Wheatons. Presentation of certificates: estimating awards and exam passes.* **Left to right:** *Richard Lovemore, Phil Gitteridge, Martin Rich, Liz Davies, Bob Brown, Tom Dunn and Harry Sharp.*

Social Security. A number of meetings were held to discuss the government's action and its unjust consequences for the pensioners.

Local Exeter MP Ben Bradshaw was consulted in 2002 with a view to keeping the matter before MPs in parliament. He referred Anthony Wheaton also to Richard Younger-Ross, MP for Teignbridge.

By 2002 no further resolution could be secured without taking legal action which was not considered a viable option.

About 800 Pergamon/BPCC Group staff members, including some at Wheatons who had not reached normal retirement date by 26 June 1992, lost 50% of their pension entitlement.

In uncertain times following the breakup of MCC and BPCC, there were a number of changes in senior management at Wheatons.

By 1995 Wheatons had become the 'star' company in the BPCC Science and Information Group. Sales from the Exeter production companies rose to £12.6 million returning management profit of £1.194 million with 341 staff. Angus Clark left Wheatons in November 1995 to become CEO of T J International – Padstow.

1996 Early in the year Divisional Finance Director, David Beattie was reappointed as Managing Director on a holding basis. Later Dr John Horrocks was appointed Managing Director.

1994 – 1998 Wheatons continued successfully without major change or direction during these years but faced increasing price competition in their markets.

1998 Tony Hall became Managing Director.

Educational Publishing – Highlights from the Backlist

From the 1950s to the 1970s Wheatons published a number of successful long running series which were used by many schools throughout the UK.

The 1963 Catalogue of School Books listed some 180 series and individual titles. In later years the list was considerably further developed.

Wheaton Education

- Early learning and reading books Mollie Clarke was a schools inspector with Devon County Council and a Wheaton author. Among her titles were: The Little Bears series, Spring, Summer, Autumn and Winter series, I Can Read a Story series, Workbooks, Little Things.
- Basis science series of 48 titles
- Happy Trio Reading Scheme, an extensive series published under licence from Scott Foresman in the USA
- Real Life Geography series by L R Hawkes
- Read About It series of 108 titles by O B Gregory
- Secondary School Atlases (with adapted editions for overseas) edited by C Midgely. These were reworked by the Pergamon Cartographic Department with S Knight as General Editor
- *Atlas of British and World History* edited by T A Rennard

- *Modern Teaching Atlas* edited by C K Brampton
- Explore and Report series by R J Mayer and D H W Thomas
- The Good Stories series by W G Lamb

Other series and many individual titles made up the list.

Juta Publishing of Johannesburg were a major customer for titles adapted for South African schools but published with their imprint. Also, Wheatons printed Juta's 400 page *English–Afrikaans dictionary* almost annually for over 15 years.

Arnold-Wheaton

- *Tricolore* was a secondary-level French course originally for lower secondary (aged 11–14) and then extended for

The wind that blew too much
WHEATON OF EXETER
REAL LIFE GEOGRAPHIES
BOOK THREE
STRANGE THINGS
Wheaton – Pergam
SECONDARY
SCHOOL
ATLAS
A Big Book
About Little Bear
by
Mollie Clarke
WHEATON · EXETER
THE "READ ABOUT IT" SERIES
BOOK 55
Hedgehogs
by
EILEEN EVERETT
A. WHEATON & CO. LTD., EXETER
ELEPHANT'S
SECOND BUSY BOOK
By MOLLIE CLARKE
WHEATON OF EXETER
O.B. GREGOR
WHEATON
LITTLE THINGS No. 7
THE KIND CROCODILE
Rubb
O.B. GREGOR
WHEATON

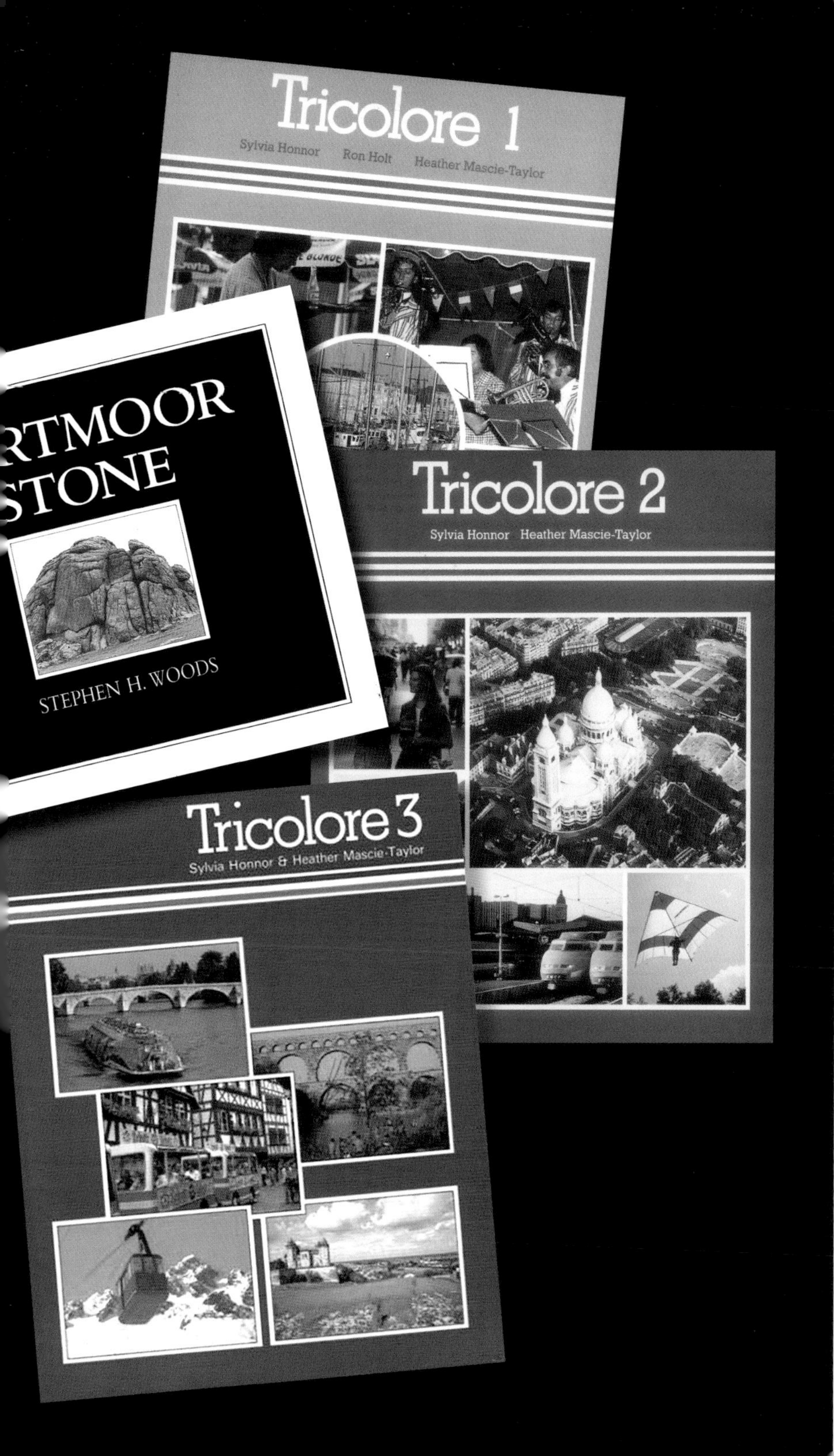

upper secondary to GCSE. It was the most successful French course for the UK and was the market leader for many years. Millions of children have used *Tricolore* in its original and subsequent editions over more than 35 years.

First published in 1980 by Arnold-Wheaton of Leeds (in association with the Nuffield Foundation) *Tricolore* was an innovative multi-component course with pupils' textbooks, teachers' books, flash cards, worksheet masters, reading cards, games cards, audio tapes/cassettes and film strips. Printed at Wheatons, *Tricolore 1* textbooks reprinted four times in the first year of publication.

By 1989 Arnold-Wheaton had been acquired by educational publishers Nelson which then became Nelson Thornes. *Tricolore* was then re-edited and launched as *Encore Tricolore*. By 2010 it was extended to GCSE with *Tricolore Total*. OUP acquired Nelson Thornes in 2013 and re-edited *Tricolore* again by 2016. The series is now in its fifth edition.

The series is centred on La Rochelle in west France. Generations of school children have since been taken on holiday to the area leading to the original authors, Sylvia Honnor and Heather Mascie-Taylor, receiving an award for tourism development.

QH
TOTAL QUALITY
TOTAL SERVICE
2010
FUEL PUMPS
POMPES À ESSENCE
KRAFTSTOFFPUMPE
BOMBAS DE COMBUSTIB
POMPE CARBURAN
BRANDSTOF OPVOER PO
R.E.D. MusicMaster 2000 DELETIONS
Centres, Bureaux & Research Institutes
the directory of UK concentrations of effort, information and expertise
Edition 4
CBD Research Publication
willings Press Guide
126th EDITION
NEW EDITION
LONDON CENTRAL AREA
A-Z
The Marketing Manager's Yearbook 2000
events
motivate
rewards
award fulfilment
performance solutions
creative communications
inspire
Including Marketing Profiles of Major UK Companies and Providers of Marketing Services
CIM The Chartered Institute of Marketing
AP
NATIONAL FARES MANUAL 75
28 May 2000 – 23 September 2000 or until further notice
MID
D&B Dun & Bradstreet
Who Owns Whom
Who Owns Wh
2000
BRAD
July 2000
CHAMBERS AND PARTNERS
CHAMBERS GLOBAL
THE WORLD'S LEADING LAWYERS
2000-2001
Miller Freeman UK is now
United Business Media
www.unitedbusinessmedia.com
and
eBusinessMedia
www.ebusinessmedia.com
Healthcare
Music
Travel
Agriculture
Building
Ingredients
Entertainment Technology
Fire/Health & Safety/Security
Print/Packaging
Interiors
June 2010
Car Values 1999-2010
GLASS GUIDE .co.uk
5 COUNTRIES 7 CENTRES
DALRY
DUBLIN
MALLUSK
PORTADOWN
QUEENSFERRY
STRATFORD-UPON-AVON
TELFORD
WILSONS
Call today on 0151 350 1200

The Polestar Era

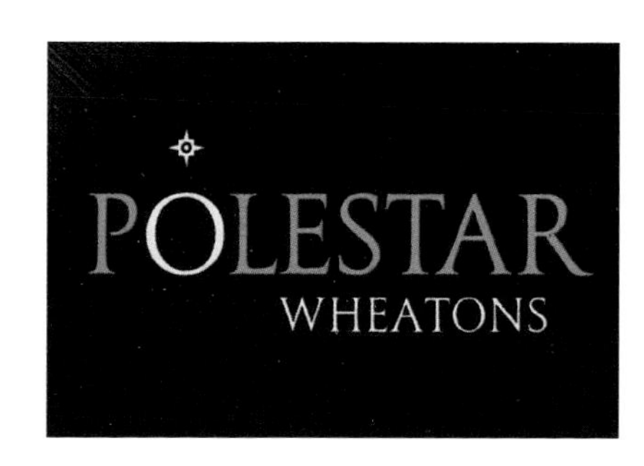

By 1998 John Holloran, formerly chief executive of MCC, together with colleagues, acquired BPCC and Watmoughs Holdings PLC from the MCC Group by way of a leveraged buyout deal backed by Bahrain-based Investcorp. The buyout embraced 27 or 28 UK printing companies including Wheatons and several in Europe.

The new Group was initially called Webinvest but later in the year they changed the name to Polestar.

The Chief Executive was Tony Rudston. On his retirement in 2001 Barry Hibbert became Group CEO.

1998 Polestar restructured the Group into operating divisions.

The previous BPCC Journals & reference Book Division from 1990 became the Special Products Group under the umbrella of the Polestar Scientifica Division, comprising the companies shown below.

Polestar Wheatons Exeter Ltd

- Polestar Aberdeen Ltd (previously Aberdeen University Press – AUP)
- Polestar Whitefriars Ltd in Tonbridge
- Polestar Digital Techset Ltd in Exeter *
- Polestar Exeter Bindery Ltd *
- Polestar Scientifica Studio Ltd in Exeter. *

The companies marked * above had previously been production departments within Wheatons and continued to operate from the Exeter site.

At Exeter conventional typesetting continued to decline. Scientific work was increasingly being received from publishers in computer format as press ready files. Polestar Digital Techset announced a further 24 redundancies in a cost cutting exercise.

Later in the year Managing Director Tony Hall received devastating notification from Reed Elsevier that they would be progressively outsourcing all of their future technical typesetting to companies in India.

However, printing of the journals would continue with Wheatons. Completed pages would be downloaded via the internet to Wheatons' pre-press file reception studio. All the company had to do was to impose the files for digital production or plate making for litho printing with no further involvement required.

Following development tests, it was apparent that the procedure would work extremely well. This change in working practices ultimately brought about the rundown and closure of Techset with the unfortunate redundancy of all remaining staff.

The closure marked the end of typesetting at Wheatons, some 68 years after the first Monotype keyboards and metal type casters were installed at Fore Street in 1930.

EPC-Dublin had also closed for similar reasons in about 1996. Some of the Bedford technical typesetting equipment was purchased from the receivers by managers and some staff. They set up a smaller company in the Dublin docklands financial district and continued working for American and Dutch publishers.

2000 The Marsh Barton Trading Estate became the centre for the motor trade and car sale showrooms for Exeter and the wider area. Part of Wheatons' site which had been sold earlier had already been developed as motor trade showrooms.

Wheatons were nominated Print Week 2000 Catalogue Printer of the Year.

2001 Bob Brown, a longstanding Wheaton employee, was made Managing Director. He continued in office for the next seven years bringing welcome stability to the company and positive planning and development for the future.

Wheatons installed their first digital press, a Heidleberg/Kodak NexPress, for short run, colour digital work.

2003 Wheatons reassessed their market and future scope. Maintaining the company's reputation as printers of reference publications, the main opportunity, apart from technical and professional books, was identified as large pagination trade directories, timetables and colour catalogues, reducing dependence on publishers' books.

Working with book publishers always involved having to accept lengthy credit terms of 60, 90 or 120 days which was a custom in the trade, particularly with the larger publishers. The publishers relied on using the printer's cash to help fund their own businesses. Once a book was published, and if successful, sales flowed in enabling the publisher to have funds to pay the printer. If the publisher's book sales were disappointing, the printer could be forced to give even more credit.

The publisher, however, had to pay the bookshop trade one third of the published price, by way of a discount, under the 'net book agreement' dating back to the 1920s. Also, bookshops would usually buy from the publisher on a sale or return basis, meaning that the publisher would be at risk of stock being returned. If dealing with the large wholesalers or supermarket chains as an alternative to the book trade, the publisher would have to discount the published price by 40–50% to secure contracts.

In the trade directory market, however, commercial credit terms of 30 days was the norm. This represented far less of the printer's working capital being tied up.

The three remaining web offset presses were ageing and mono sheet fed litho printing for bookwork was becoming uncompetitive except for shorter runs. Mono book printing for general publishers was overly competitive and was gravitating to the few remaining UK book printing groups.

Academic book production in hard case binding style continued mainly for the Elsevier academic imprint, the Wheaton Book Plan service and for other professional publishers.

Over the years, the company used Smyth-Horne, Martini, Muller Martini, Kolbus 36 and Kolbus 40 binding plant for hard cased production and flexi cover books.

2004 A developer approached the company on behalf of Vauxhall with a proposition to acquire the factory area for motor trade development and offered to build Wheatons a new factory elsewhere. The company was already beginning to outgrow the by now ageing premises and the opportunity to plan a more modern factory was favourably considered.

The offer from the developer was to build a new factory on land adjacent to the M5 motorway near junction 28 at Cullompton. The plan never progressed beyond the evaluation stage as Polestar did not follow it up.

By 2004 the Elsevier journal programme had increased to some 220 titles, with about 30 from non-Group publishers. Elsevier were requiring increased use of colour for graphics and illustrations in journals. At about this time Elsevier established a journals production unit of their own in the centre of Exeter employing some 15 staff.

The digital age and use of the internet were developing rapidly.

At this time, Wheatons were running three Rachwal camera-ready copy (CRC) to plate making systems providing a very significant increase in productivity and litho plate making capacity.

By now, apart from three web offset presses, the company had installed more large format sheet-fed colour presses to include one KBA Rapida A1 8-unit press and one Roland 700 B1 6-unit press in addition to the ex-Arnold Roland 800 AO 4-unit press installed in mid-1985. However, much of this plant was ageing.

After much discussion with current customers and potential customers, management identified more modern production plant best suited to enable Wheatons to shift further into the trade directory and information publication market and to offer an increasingly specialised and competitive service.

Discussions followed with senior directors of Polestar to show what the team at Wheatons believed would be achieved in terms of financial returns and how the business could be rejuvenated with phased new plant investment.

The Operations Director, Richard Lovemore, and Print Manager, Gary Brereton, had identified that to speed up operational requirements there was a need to change from computer to film to computer to plate. The proposal was approved by Barry Hibbert, Polestar's Chief Executive Officer (CEO) and an agreement was signed with Agfa at the IPEX, the printing industry's exhibition, to supply the relevant upgrades and equipment.

To print covers quickly enough and of the required quality there was also a need to replace two older printing machines. Once financial agreements had been obtained, a Heidelberg SM74 B2 format colour press was ordered. Both of these investments brought immediate benefits to production times, quality and payback.

It was known that web press manufacturer, Timson Engineering Co, had a revolutionary Zero Make-Ready (ZMR) book press already in production at several printing companies around the world. After discussions with all other potential web press manufacturers, it was agreed that, with a little tweaking, the Timson ZMR T48 best suited the company's needs. Discussion with Timson went well and visits to several sites in the USA and in Europe were arranged for Gary Brereton, Don Andrews, the Engineering Manager, and Bob Brown. It soon became clear that this press, together with a new binding plant, would take Wheatons to a much higher level. At that time there was no other printer in the UK offering such specialised services. The Timson would provide more capacity than the old webs, a much better schedule adherence, together with much improved quality and profitability through more cost effective working.

What was not known at this time was that Reed Elsevier, the company's largest customer, were already working with a company in France that had just installed a Timpson press to print books and journals. Elsevier were very supportive of Wheatons' proposal to install a Timson and were helpful in arranging a visit to the French printer. The company's number one customer was now on board.

A presentation was made to the Polestar Board for the purchase of the Timson ZMR. This went well and, after many questions, Barry Hibbert, Group Chief Executive Officer, agreed that the proposal to purchase the press should move forward. However, as the price was between £2.5 and £3 million, it would have to go before the Investcorp Board. Bob Brown and Shaun Lee, the Finance Director, subsequently made a presentation at an Investcorp Board meeting in London. After a two-hour presentation and questions, Investcorp gave the go ahead for an early order to be placed.

The next proposed investment was in the bindery, to replace the two ageing hotmelt glue binding lines with a state-of-the-art, fast make-ready, quick running machine. After visits to all of the major suppliers and visits by senior Polestar directors, Richard Lovemore, Operations Director, and Dave Lippit, Bindery Manager, and his bindery team recommended the Muller Martini Bolero.

It was with great credit to all of the staff who worked on this machine that, after training in Exeter and in Switzerland, changes to working practices and some heartache, the Bolero produced everything that was hoped for.

Coupled with the proposed plan which would greatly increase capacity and quality, was a need to increase sales and retain all current customers. Graham Durrant was recruited from a major UK book printing company and appointed Sales Director.

2004 As a result of the research and presentations Polestar and Investcorp approved an overall £6.1 million reinvestment programme to include:

- A Timson T48 ZMR A4-A5-A6 format 2-unit heatset web offset press to produce 48 and 64 page folded sections in mono or 2-colour
- A Heidleberg SM74 B2 5-unit sheet-fed printing press
- A Muller Martini Bolero PUR glue perfect binding line with 27 section feeder stations capable of binding publications up to and over 1,200 pages in one pass, with book trimming to final format inline
- Two computer to plate automatic digital plate making systems as upgrades from Agfa.

Also new digital equipment would be leased:

- An Oce VarioStream 9210 digital web imaging line for short run mono journals and bookwork
- A Hewlett Packard Indigo 3250 6-colour digital web imaging line to provide colour for short run journal production and other work.

The Timson ZMR and the Muller Martini Bolero were the first installations of these machines in the UK. These highly productive machines gave the company the capacity to address mainstream UK and European markets mainly for A4, A5 and A6 formats in directories, catalogues, plant lists, timetables and similar work at much improved productivity.

General publishers, standard formats of Royal, Demy, Crown Quarto and B format paperbacks were not economically catered for on the Timpson.

Prior consultations with company union chapels in advance of these investments went well and morale became good throughout the company.

The Timson ZMR web press and Bolero binder were installed. These state-of-the-art new machines involved the use of computer-based set up and running routines. Key shift leaders, having attended manufacturers' training courses, had now to become technicians and it naturally took time for the full scope of productivity improvements to develop.

To reduce interruptions in production, close scheduling and monitoring of work flows were necessary. This involved all departments from the production office, through the file reception studio and digital

Non-stop press to Exeter

Wheatons paves way with Timson ZMR

By Gareth Ward

Polestar Wheatons is to be the first in the UK with Timsons' revolutionary ZMR T48A press.

The Kettering press manufacturer has already sold ten of the book presses worldwide to customers in France and Italy as well as eight to the US.

The press can switch from one job to another in a matter of seconds without stopping and leaving just a few feet of paper as waste. It works by having a second perfecting unit plated up and ready. When the preset number of copies is close to completion, the new cylinders accelerate to press speed and in one move the plates on the first unit are sprung off and the cylinders with the new plates drop on.

The impact on Wheatons will be just as dramatic. Its current web press capacity is based on heatset Solnas and a Harris V15, both producing 16pp sections while the Timson will produce 48pp.

These will be bound in the Müller Martini Bolero currently being installed at the Exeter factory. Says managing director Bob Brown: "We will have the very best web printing and limp binding facilities the industry can offer."

The Timson is configured to be able to print two colours and will arrive in March. "It should be running by the end of April," says Mr Brown.

"It continues the radical changes that have been going on in our business. Over the last three years we've had a completely new prepress with three ctp systems. We have digital presses, both colour and black and white and now the most productive web press. I don't think that anybody will have anything with this firepower."

Timsons has sold a conventional T48A to Clowes for its new factory in a similar information products market, but not the ZMR version and last week sold another to Bookmarque the Fulmar subsidiary.

gward@cmpinformation.com

Summary

- Wheatons to pioneer non-stop press
- Boosts web production capacity
- Unrivalled firepower to company

Printing World | August 5 2004

2004. *The Chairman of Timson Engineering with Bob Brown*

plate making, to ensure a constant flow of printing plates to the press and afterwards marshalling folded sections for jobs for the bindery. This also took time to perfect for successful 24-hour operation.

On visits by potential new customers, the Timson ZMR was an impressive sight. Running mono work at 18,000 folded sections per hour without stopping for plate changes or paper reel changes and running 24-hours a day for five days a week – no visitor would have seen such a productive press before.

In the bindery, the Bolero line collated up to over 1,200 page publications without pre-collates and delivered finished bound copies at 8,000 or 4,000 units per hour (depending on format) ready for packing and dispatch the same day.

Important and long-standing new accounts were progressively added during 2004 and following years, including those shown below.

- British Rail national fare manuals
- *Glass's Guide* motor trade price guide
- Vauxhall parts list supplies catalogue
- Arvin motor exhaust systems catalogues
- *National Farm Manual*
- Dunn & Bradstreet catalogues.

2006 *Muller Martini's award of a large Swiss cow bell and banner for the 'best use of the Bolero binder in the UK' (the cow bell was later displayed in Wheatons' reception for a number of years).*

Left to Right: *Peter Schoeneberg; Finance Director, The Muller Martini Sales Director, Richard Lovemore; Operations Director, Bob Brown; Managing Director and Dave Lippett; Bindery Manager.*

2004 *Wheatons bindery staff attend a training course on the Bolero binding line at Felben, Switzerland.*

As press forward loadings built up there was little spare capacity. Prior liaison with customers had to be precise to ensure on time availability for their jobs.

The print runs were sometimes more than 100 hours printing (in the order of 180,000 copies). If jobs were late it left a gap as the next customer's job would not yet be ready. Such lost production was costly with standing press crews. To help counter this, 'filler' work was arranged which could be drawn forward at any time and held as bound stock for call off by the publisher when needed. Useful accounts were developed with puzzle book publisher, Millard and others.

In four years the management team shown below had changed the face of the business.

Managing Director
Bob Brown

Sales Director
Graham Durrant

Finance Director
Shaun Lee

Operations Director
Richard Lovemore

Print Manager
Gary Brereton

Assistant Print Manager
Neil Whittaker

Bindery Manager
Dave Lippit

Engineering Manager
Don Andrew

Factory Facilities Manager
Dale Buckingham

Customer Services Manager
Paul Cummings

There were special acknowledgements to Mike Walmsley, a main board member of Polestar, who was very supportive of Wheatons' proposals.

2005 In December at the annual Polestar Star Awards ceremony at Alton Towers, Wheatons was awarded overall winner – Polestar Company of the Year, having won three of the eight top awards.

The citation read 'With this award, the teamwork and enthusiasm of the staff and management – plus a healthy dose of hard work – play a large part in the successful company's accolade. All of these elements have contributed to Polestar Wheatons receiving this award, but there are some specific achievements that have also provided the winning formula for its success. A 30% increase on 2004 in EBITDA [Earnings before interest, tax, depreciation and amortization, a measure of a company's performance] keeps everybody happy, and this has been achieved alongside the installation of a new web press, the start of NVQ training for the company's customer service team, health and safety training involving all employees'.

A Group Star Award to employees for best technician of the year went to Peter Bates who had been a major contributor in getting the Timson ZMR into production. Peter had been with the company for 20 years, having started work as an apprentice. The 'unsung hero' award went to twins Kay Smalldon and Nicky Ayre who worked in the bindery on the sewing machines. They worked tirelessly in support of the new demanding production schedules.

Polestar was creative in encouraging employees to develop their full potential. The Group ran inter-company and company team building events.

In 2003 the Polestar Group long service award had been handed to David Lee, an invoicing clerk with 46 years' service. He had joined Wheatons at the age of 15 in the Works Study Office at 143 Fore Street.

As was the case in earlier years, employee service with the company of 30, 40 or even 50 years was not unusual. Many staff joined as apprentices and worked nowhere else and some had sons, daughters or other relatives working for the company.

Wheatons, with its activities in publishing, printing, bookselling and stationery, school and library supplies until 1991, was well known in Exeter. Many Exeter people knew somebody who worked for the company.

Wheatons' 2005 annual sales were by now in excess of £12 million on which the company made a management profit of £1.7 million, up from £1 million in 2004.

1998 The Polestar Challenge – Scotland
Left to right: Bob Brown, Richard Lovemore, Mike Greenslade, Phil Gutteridge, Mr. Brass, (husband of Monica Brass, Accounts) Colin Goodwin, Les Cox, Ian Knapper and Adrian Walters

2000 Tottenham versus Middlesbrough White Hart Lane
Left to right: Gerald Richardson, (Finance Director) Bob Brown (Sales Director) and Andrew Wright (Head of print procurement at Reed Elsevier)

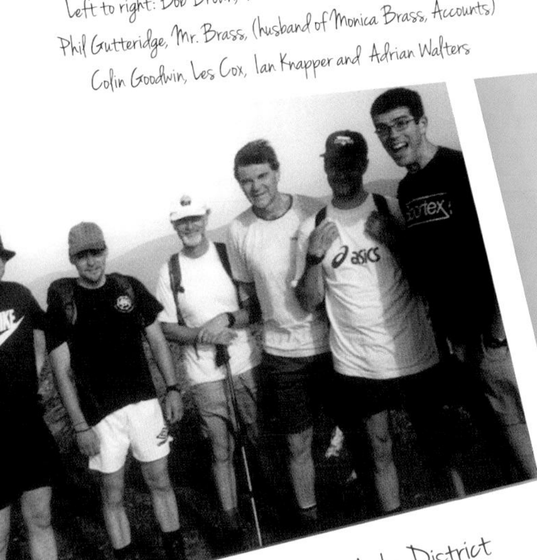

2000 The Polestar Challenge – Lake District
Left to right: Richard Hinchliffe, Dave Richards, Adrian Walters, Bob Brown and Gary Marchant

2000 Fun Run – Bovey Tracey
Left to right: David Lee, Harry Sharp, Richard Lovemore and Bob Brown.

With the benefit of new technologies and with factory productivity much improved, fewer staff were required. The printing departments now employed fewer than 150 staff.

2006 Polestar had become the UK's largest printing group with 40–45% of the UK consumer magazine market and printing 50 million magazine units per week.

Polestar Group companies not associated with the magazine market no longer fitted logically within the Group and this included Wheatons. Polestar began seeking a buyer for the company. Exploratory talks took place with one of the few remaining large UK book printing groups. A price could not be agreed and no sale proceeded.

The Polestar Group sales person of the year was awarded to Richard Hinchliffe, the Sales Manager at Wheatons.

2007 Andrew Lee was appointed Managing Director. Wheatons employed 138 staff in printing and binding including digital production. Publishing, typesetting, retail and stationery departments had all closed or been sold off.

2007–2009 were profitable years. Company sales rose to £12.5 million with annual management profits in the order of £1 million to £1.5 million. By now Wheatons were being encouraged to accept more work from their main customers and further sales prospects were identified. Wheatons were often not large enough to take advantage of these opportunities.

Wheatons attained the following environmental credentials as responsible employers and to aid customer confidence in the company:

- ISO 14001 – environmental management
- ISO 9001 – quality management
- Forest Stewardship Council (FSC)/ Programme for the Endorsement of Forest Certification (PEFC) – sustainable paper chain of custody
- Alcohol free printing – near zero volatile organic compounds contributing to low level ozone
- 22 recycling streams
- Sedex – approval in part. Social and ethical sourcing data exchange for supply chains to allow working with organisations such as Fairtrade, Bodyshop, Oxfam and others.

Several years' later talks took place to consider an acquisition by Polestar of another long established West Country book printer with a view to merging the business with Wheatons. Talks proceeded to due diligence stage but concluded without agreement.

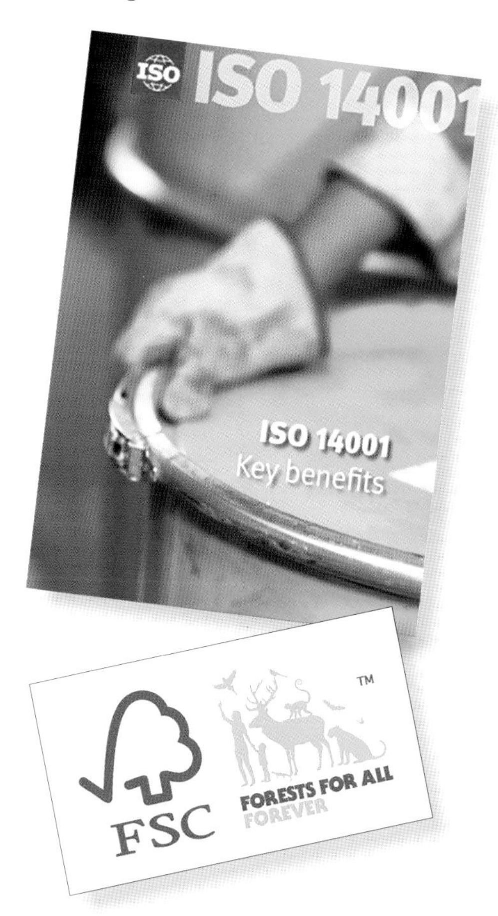

2010 The management team at this time is shown below.

Managing Director
Andrew Lee

Sales Director
Andrew Keighley

Operations Director
David Thompson

Finance Director
Peter Schoeneberg

Manufacturing and Prepress
Operations Manager
Neil Whittaker

Prepress Manager
Mark Ellis

Bindery Manager
Dave Lippit

Digital Production Manager
Ben Lay

Commercial Manager
Geoffrey Dolan

Estimating Manager
Steve Ottley

Customer Care Manager
Laura Burgess

The company's large format sheet-fed litho printing machines for colour work were ageing. A study commenced to evaluate more modern presses.

In spite of Polestar's serious financial problems a proposal was approved to install a Manroland 700 HiPrint 10-unit press at a cost of £1.7 million. This state-of-the-art press with computer control systems, auto plate changing and a pumped ink system would replace three older machines.

The press would provide 4-colour backed up and sealed A1 or B1 sheets to high print quality, running at a production rate of 8,000–12,000 sheets per hour. The press showed a 20% saving on previous colour printing costs. The purchase was commuted to a lease agreement.

The Manroland 700 was installed in 2011. Working on two shifts, the press accommodated most of Wheatons' colour printing needs and undertook some Group work for other Polestar companies.

In the period 2000 to 2010, and as the digital age became established, the UK printing industry in all market sectors experienced a rate of technical change and decline not seen before. Many well-known printing companies were forced to close including members of the Polestar Group. In the industry as a whole:

- Newspapers and magazine sales began falling year-on-year as viewing on the internet became an alternative to print. Also, younger people were progressively reading fewer newspapers.
- Journal print runs reduced progressively. Subscription publications could be viewed online and required articles or papers extracted.
- The internet and secure file transfer procedures of PDFs enabled publishers to print anywhere in the world making use of lower cost markets.
- Printed directories and information publications in printed form were declining slowly. Online versions of the same titles were becoming available.
- Non-time sensitive publications continued to be printed more economically overseas.
- Some titles became published as internet editions only.
- Commercial print continued. However, catalogues and brochures were selectively migrating to alternative, more versatile digital production.
- Direct marketing via the internet, by e-mail and personalised mailings was increasingly becoming the way forward.

- Production orders could be produced digitally on demand in small quantities and topped up when more were required.
- Educational books were giving way to computer-based learning material. The tipping point for many publishers of 50% print, 50% computer-based resources had already occurred.
- Desktop publishing enabled authors to key their own work and make up pages. No trade typesetting was required. Self-publishing was growing.
- E-books could be downloaded eliminating the need for a printed copy.
- Smart phones enabled information with good quality pictures to be instantly obtained from almost anywhere.

2011 The Polestar Group overall was close to financial collapse. New funding was arranged from Sun Capital Partners (Europe and USA).

The Group pension fund had liabilities of £45 million which Sun Capital Partners would not accommodate. The pension scheme was hived off and entered the Government Pension Protection Fund which guaranteed members 90% of their pension entitlements.

Sales Director, Andrew Keighley left the company to be replaced by Anthony Rowell.

At the British Book Awards ceremony Wheatons were announced as the winner Best Digitally Printed Book 2011.

Previous Company Production Department member, Peter Leach, who had gone on to an extensive career with a major book production group and had run his own business, re-joined Wheatons as Operations Director.

Production was increasingly concentrated on the Timson ZMR and the new Manroland 7 10-unit colour press. Older, less productive presses were sold and staff numbers reduced.

The scientific, academic and medical journal programme comprised monthly, bi-monthly and quarterly published titles. In the 1980s, then published by Pergamon, the average print run was 1,000–3,000 copies and 160 pages printed batch production web offset. By 2007, under Elsevier, the print runs had reduced to 250–300 copies with paginations of 32–300 pages produced digitally. Remaining longer runs from 1,000–1,500 were printed batch production on the Timson ZMR. Over the years, the number of titles increased as many journals split into more specialised subject areas.

2012 Disaster struck! Following extensive negotiations, which finally proved unsuccessful, Elsevier served notice to terminate their contract with the company for their, by now, 480 journal titles.

The journals programme represented one of the mainstays of Wheatons. The profitable sales originating from the days of Pergamon, had continued for 40 years.

Wheatons' service, prices, quality and attention to customer needs were not in question. Some prices were even reduced to suit the customer. Elsevier had for years used three suppliers for their European journals programme: one in Holland, Henry Ling in Dorset and Wheatons. Everything had been done to ensure that Wheatons' services matched the needs of Elsevier. In 2011 the digital production plant was upgraded to an HP 7250 6-colour web press which at 18,000 impressions per hour, was four times faster than the previous HP 3250. A higher quality HP Indigo 5500 for cover printing was added. Single colour journals to larger page extents and runs above 500 copies were already well catered for by batch production on the Timson ZMR.

The issue was that the Production Manager at Elsevier (not long in post) needed to reduce the number of suppliers from three to two. Wheatons lost out. The underlying weak financial position of Polestar may have been a consideration.

Elsevier would have been mindful that their titles would continue to become more specialised in their fields. Journal issues would be of fewer pages as internet delivery on reader subscription to specific research material was a growing alternative to print production. Wheatons had not developed such fulfilment services.

However, it was agreed that the 480 journal titles would be transferred on a phased basis to the other suppliers over a two-year period.

Ironically, the Dutch supplier subsequently ran into financial difficulties. Elsevier came back to Wheatons seeking assistance and asked Wheatons to take on extra titles, temporarily bringing the total to 520 journals. Later the Dutch supplier overcame its difficulties and the transfer from Wheatons resumed.

Sales efforts were launched to backfill the loss from other scientific publishers but at short notice, without success. The digital production department and the dedicated journals bindery were run down with resultant staff redundancies. The office administrative Journals Production Unit (JPU) was closed.

With the benefit of the higher quality HP 7250 digital colour press, the company began to offer a service for publishers of books with colour where a short run service would be relevant. Titles could be batched together and queued to the HP for flow-line production. Some success was achieved.

By late 2014 the loss of the journals across the company (representing some 80% of the workload of the digital department) was to force the company into a loss-making position, meaning that Wheatons were no longer making a positive contribution to Polestar's earnings. However, for a further three years Polestar, in spite of being in serious financial difficulties themselves, continued to financially support Wheatons whilst significant economies in staffing and overheads were made. Meanwhile Polestar were seeking a buyer for the company. It was deemed a better option to keep the company going rather than to close it. The redundancy costs, lease commitments and dilapidations and other expenses could run up to £5 million.

2013 In April Managing Director Andrew Lee was transferred to a central Group role to set up a Polestar Group Commercial Department. Andrew Reynoldson became Managing Director having been transferred from within the Group. Sales Director, Anthony Rowell left the company. European Sales Manager Richard Hinchliffe took over, mainly for the directories and commercial publications market.

2014 In April Andrew Lee returned as Managing Director at Wheatons and also became Managing Director at Stones in Banbury, another Polestar company.

Polestar's financial problems continued. Since the launch of Polestar in 1998 and after being re-financed three times, 14 Group plants had been closed and three more had been sold. Overall, Group staff were by now reduced to approximately 1,500.

It was an uncertain and anxious period for all staff. Following the 2008 UK economic slowdown coupled with the contracting printing industry, salaries and wages remained static or restricted. There were very limited opportunities for the company to increase prices to customers in a declining market.

Morale was not good but most employees understood and accepted the situation in the interests of job security.

Actions continued to reduce costs and increase productivity to help reduce company losses.The main office block was progressively vacated and the Production Office was transferred to the factory premises previously occupied by Techset. The administrative offices were offered for let.

2015 Managing Director Andrew Lee left the company and his place was temporarily taken by Paul Banton from Stones.

New financial backers, Proventus, took control of Polestar from Sun Capital and became the major Group shareholder.

In November Peter Leach left the company.

Management and staff were becoming disillusioned by events within Polestar and a lack of direction for Wheatons. New investment plans to address the evolving digital market needed consideration but were not possible.

2016 In January Polestar appointed Tony Chard as Managing Director at Wheatons. He had experience of senior executive roles in the industry and came with an in-depth knowledge of the digital production process. He had been a Sales Manager with BPCC some years earlier and had originally worked at Wheatons in 1994. His first priority was to stabilise the company, reassure the staff and keep the business trading.

Neil Whittaker, a long-standing employee of the company and Manufacturing Manager, was appointed Operations Director.

The Production Office team and managers committed to stay together to help retain customers and maintain value in the business whilst a buyer was sought.

Administrators, Pricewaterhouse-Coopers (PwC), were appointed at five remaining Polestar companies.

For the second time, Polestar entered into a 'pre-pack' sale administration process (see page129) to Proventus to protect the Group from creditors and avoid liabilities.

After the 'pre-pack' sale, Polestar's largest customer, DMG Media, publishers of the *Daily Mail,* declined to transfer their account to the 'new' Polestar. Two other major customers were also lost. After one month Polestar was unable to continue trading. Administrators were again appointed to sell the remaining companies as going concerns or to sell their assets on closures.

In May it was announced that Group Chief Executive Officer, Barry Hibbert, had left Polestar under arrangements with the Administrator. A few months earlier he had made a reassuring visit to Wheatons.

Stones and Wheatons were offered for sale together as Stones-Wheatons.

Wheatons worked hard to retain their key customers. Some customers were lost, fearful that their work could be trapped or delayed if the company was to close.

The Digital Department, now without the journals, was underemployed and could not be commercially sustained. The leased HP 7250 digital production line was removed and the department downsized. The rundown of the Digital Department, though necessary to save costs, was unfortunate as it possessed, albeit perhaps without the appropriate equipment, the experience and culture from which future digital services could develop.

The Goss 'Sunday 5000' 96 page press

Polestar's UK Plan

Polestar never quite achieved its master objective. Over 13 years successive investors – Investec, Sun Capital and Proventus had all identified that there was a recognisable business plan for a core business which was plausible.

By 1999 Polestar had decided to specialise in national colour magazines and newspaper colour supplement printing contracts and had begun building up market share with the view to becoming dominant in this field.

By 2012 the Magazine Division had secured some 45% of the market, producing 50 million copies per week. Working at low prices in a declining market, Polestar maintained crushing pressure on their competitors, a number of whom were forced out of business. Polestar's strategy was to increase market share to over 50%, at which point and beyond competition could fall away. Polestar could then progressively ramp up production with new modern plant, lift prices and return to profitability.

So far Polestar's production plants were equipped with similar 32-page and 64-page web offset presses to their competitors'. With new investment backing available, Polestar would invest in state-of-the-art, larger and more productive equipment to outperform UK competition. Meanwhile, some existing Group magazine plants would be integrated, downsized or closed in a cost reduction exercise. In a falling market the new printing presses would not represent an increase in Group capacity as older presses would be decommissioned. Polestar's technical team took a year to select the most relevant new technology and to work with the chosen supplier.

A new factory was built at Sheffield alongside the existing gravure plant (printing high quality, long run magazines). At a cost of £50 million the new site was to be equipped initially with two Goss 96-page presses and a 64-page press. The site was to be referred to by Chief Executive Officer, Barry Hibbert, as 'the powerhouse of the north'.

In fact six new presses were ordered in 2013 from Goss International. These were two 96-page Sunday 5000 presses, two 64-page Sunday 4000 presses and two 16-page M600 cover presses with associated finishing equipment. The presses were to be installed, mostly at Sheffield, in 2014 and 2015, with some being considered for other Polestar plants.

The 96-page presses were the first machines of this type to be installed in the UK.

Production started with the first 96-page press late in 2014 – but there had been extensive technical problems delaying the start up for almost a year.

In the meantime, in addition to current contracts, Polestar had won a large new

An alternative view of the Goss 'Sunday 5000' press

account – Time Life Publications UK. Without the expected extra printing capacity on time, work had to be outsourced at considerable extra cost to avoid breaching contract terms with customers. There were to be financial consequences for the Group.

By December 2015 Polestar were close to running out of cash. Accountants Deloitte were brought in to advise on a new financial structure for the Group for the next three years.

New investor, Proventus, agreed a new loan facility for Polestar of up to £90 million, took control from Sun Capital and became the major Group shareholder. Proventus put in their own Chief Financial Officer and four of their own directors on the Polestar Board.

Polestar's gravure Printing Division had been steadily losing sales of up to nearly £1million per month in 2014 due to the fall off in newspaper paginations and run lengths affecting colour supplements. At shorter runs, previously viable gravure work was now more economically produced by web offset, as Polestar had anticipated.

As markets declined and Polestar's consolidation continued, 13 Group companies had been closed and two others sold since 1999. Polestar commented in 2011 that a number of their main competitors in the UK had already been consolidated or gone into administration.

With growing uncertainly in the market, some publishers were removing their work from Polestar, placing it with the few remaining UK companies, or were making contingency plans with continental printers.

Polestar had reputed debts of £100 million.

In March 2016, a 'pre-pack' administration sale was organised by PricewaterhouseCoopers (PwC) to create New Polestar Ltd, viewed as a most contentious development by creditors and suppliers.

Key customers were not satisfied. Vital contracts with DMG Media – publishers of the *Daily Mail*, and two other large publishers were not renewed with New Polestar. These events, coupled with problems with trade suppliers, pushed the Group over the edge.

After one month, on 27 April 2016, administrators PwC were called in to seek a buyer for the remaining Group or its parts. PwC had already been appointed as administrators to five Polestar companies including Stones and Wheatons.

The new Sheffield web offset factory never achieved its objective. Time ran out before the benefit of the new investments could be delivered. No buyer could be found for the Sheffield site as a going concern. The web offset plant and the gravure plant ceased operation by 31 May with a loss of 548 jobs.

INSOLVENCY

NOTE: Pre-packaged insolvency, known as a 'a pre-pack', is a kind of bankruptcy procedure, where a restructure plan is agreed in advance of a company declaring its insolvency. In the United States pre-packs are often used in a Chapter 11 filing. In the United Kingdom, pre-packs have become popular since the Enterprise Act 2002, which has made administration the dominant insolvency procedure.

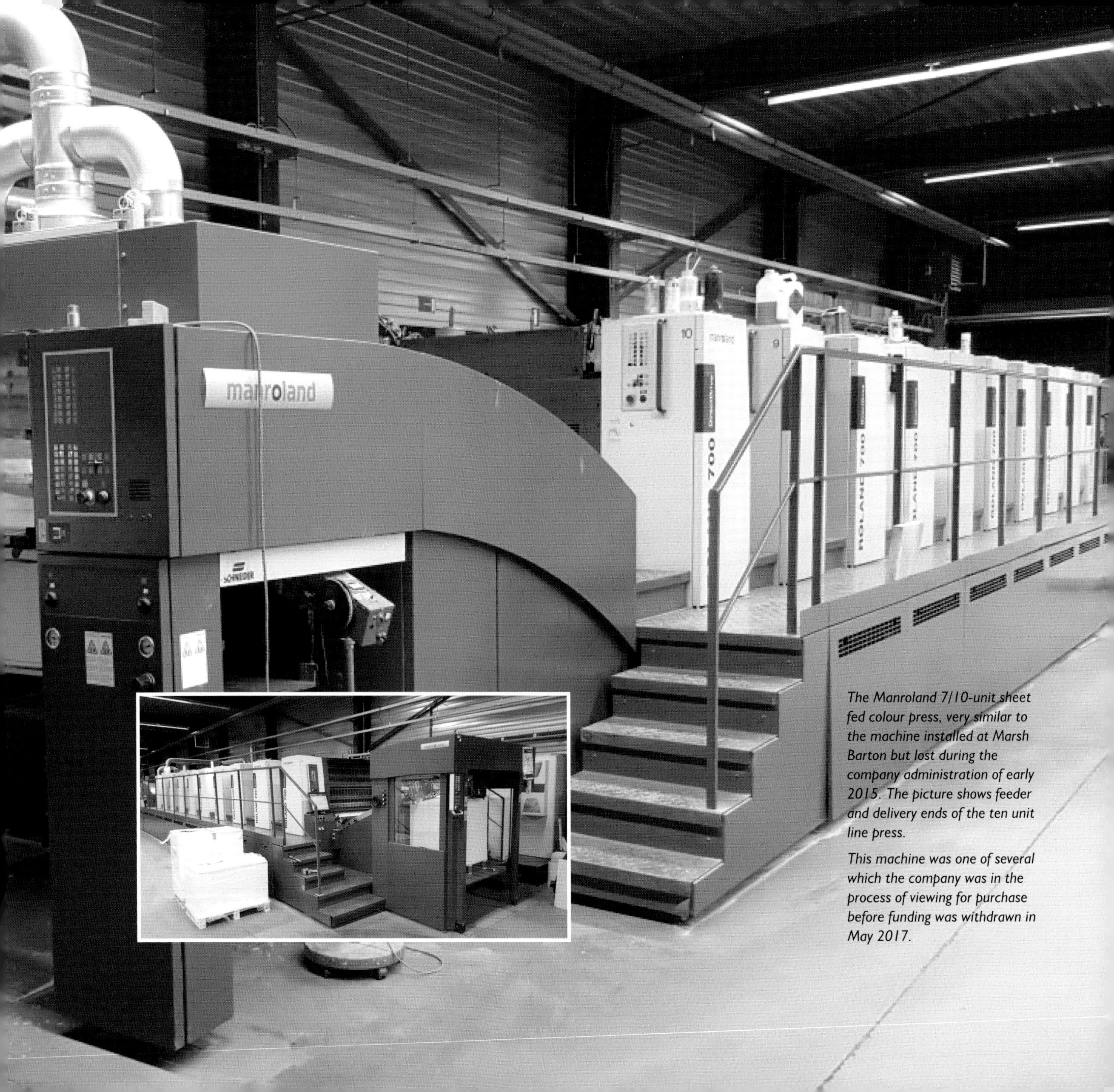

The Manroland 7/10-unit sheet fed colour press, very similar to the machine installed at Marsh Barton but lost during the company administration of early 2015. The picture shows feeder and delivery ends of the ten unit line press.

This machine was one of several which the company was in the process of viewing for purchase before funding was withdrawn in May 2017.

The Rescue Deal Initiative

On 25 April 2016 New Polestar UK Print Ltd was placed in administration. Wheatons continued to trade.

On 28 April a management buyout (MBO) team made a declaration of interest to the PwC administrator to acquire Stones-Wheatons as going concerns. They made a 'best and final offer' with a deal to be completed by 10 May.

The buyout team from both companies is shown below.

- Finance Director of both Stones and Wheatons
- Production Director at Stones
- European Sales Manager at Wheatons
- Commercial Services Manager at Wheatons
- Estimating Manager at Stones

There was a need to reduce costs in support of the proposed deal and 36 redundancies were announced.

A critical meeting followed with the landlord of the Wheatons' site to negotiate a reduction in the annual rent for the factory and to agree a new tenure of tenancy. Good progress was made. The rent was significantly reduced and dilapidations were accepted as being for the landlord. A longer tenure was agreed. The landlord realised that it would be more beneficial to help to keep the company going rather than see closure with no early tenant in prospect for the large factory.

Negotiations with the administrator became frustratingly protracted due partly to diligent valuation of all assets at both companies. No deal was finalised by 10 May deadline.

On 16 May the MBO members' offer was recommended by the administrator but had to be put to the senior secured creditor.

Late on the evening of 8 June the administrator came back and tabled a list of revised criteria in order to accept the offer. Subsequent negotiations resulted in the original offer being increased. There was no response for two days. The company came within six hours of closure with the prospect of the deal drifting away.

On 10 June terms were agreed with the administrator, and on behalf of secured creditors, for the sale of the businesses and assets with funding provided by Thames Valley Capital.

All wages and salaries continued to be paid in full.

The company's new registered name became Wheatons Exeter Ltd.

The acquisition was formally announced on 14 June to relieved staff and clients. The company went forward with 59 employees and could see its way to viability and a

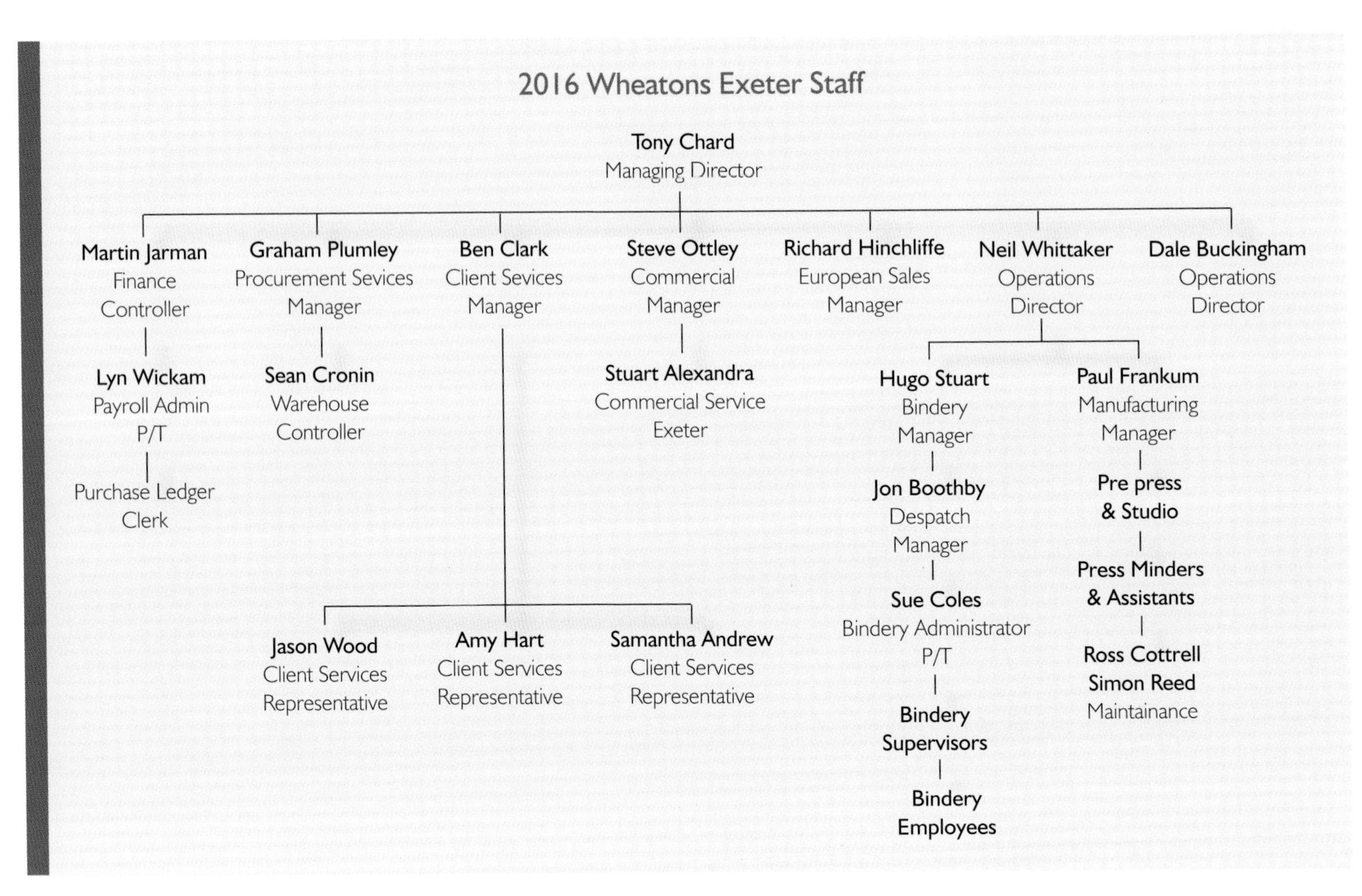

sustainable future. Remaining clients were very supportive and continuity arrangements were made with trade suppliers.

Regrettably the Manroland 7–10 colour press could not be retained due to unreasonable creditor demands and it was subsequently sold to a printer in Poland. Fortunately the company had a solution. Colour printing from Exeter would be undertaken on Stones' colour presses. Although not ideal, it was a solution for the time being, nonetheless. Also, as Stones had lost magazine cover printing work from other Polestar plants, the additional volume was welcome for them.

At last Wheatons' buyout team could make their own decisions to stabilise the company and actively plan for the future to address changing market requirements.

The Wheaton trading name continued. The new owners, in acknowledgment of the company's long history, adopted as their logo the company seal from the 1900s *(see previous page)*.

Just too many hurdles

It was always going to be a challenge for the new company to shake off the legacy of Polestar. However with £6 million of retained sales, supporting customers and suppliers and a dedicated staff, the company had a good chance although cash management would remain a concern.

Having taken over the running of the company from 11 June 2016, after being in administration for eleven weeks, the management buyout team succeeded in stabilising the business.

Crucial to their plans was the reinstatement, as soon as possible, of the 10-unit colour printing press and the associated revenues stream by bringing outsourced colour printing work back to the business. By autumn of 2016 the company was trading profitably on a month by month basis during the traditionally busy part of the year. At the same time, a significant portion of the financial loan from Thames Valley Capital was repaid by the end of the year.

Unfortunately a chain of adverse events were soon to occur. From January 2017 the company ran into its normal quiet trading period through to March which became compounded by the loss of a major annual academic book printing account. Then almost £500,000 of booked in directory production schedules for May/June was postponed until August/September leaving the factory well under-utilised.

These unexpected events created a cash flow shortage from May to August which the company could not bridge.

In the meantime, negotiations were proceeding with HMRC with regard to a rescheduling proposal to address some unpaid PAYE payments due from June to December 2016 after the buyout. It had been hoped that a phased payment plan could be agreed. The company had been up to date with PAYE for 2017. HMRC were not accommodating and eventually rejected the application and was expected to issue a winding up petition against Wheatons Exeter Ltd.

Prior to the HMRC matter the company directors had expected to arrange a bridging loan from their financial backers or their associated company. Already arranged was funding for the purchase of a replacement 10-unit printing press. Several available machines were being viewed in Europe for an immediate purchase.

In view of the cash flow shortage resulting from the loss of expected contracts and the rejection of the company's proposal to HMRC, the financial plan for the replacement press was withdrawn.

Under the circumstances, the directors concluded that in the best interests of stakeholders the company should again be placed in administration.

KRE Corporate Recovery was appointed administrators by 16 May 2017. On appointment, of the 63 staff, 23 including Managing Director Tony Chard, were made redundant. The company continued to trade whilst a possible buyer was sought. Further redundancies were announced later.

Sadly, in the event no buyer was located able to keep the business running as a going concern in Exeter. On 1 June the administrator closed the business after 237 years of trading since Mr Penny opened his bookshop in Exeter which became Wheatons in 1835.

In a most emotive moment, Operations Director Neil Whittaker, with 29 years' service with the company, was one of the last senior staff members to leave the building.

Over the years Wheatons of Exeter have manufactured many millions of books and other publications for publishers large and small – many of these books will remain out there as *'lasting impressions'*.

A litho-press printed sheet delivery

How the Book Production Market Changed

In 1986 the prolific British publishing industry launched 58,845 new and revised titles. The number of titles published had increased annually from 17,072 in 1950. Most books were conventionally printed by litho and a few still by letterpress. Flexi-cover editions were gaining ground at the expense of hard case binding.

The BPCC Book Production Group companies (including Wheatons) with sales to publishers of £34 million were collectively the largest supplier to the UK market accounting for 15.4% of book work printed in the UK.

However, 26% of publishers' output was already being placed with overseas printers at lower prices. Sheet-fed general book printing became most competitive amongst the larger traditional printers. Some small, lower cost companies, often privately owned, specialising in short runs, gained market share. Web offset mono book printing in the 3,000 to 10,000 copies range remained more viable.

In the following years it was not that the annual output of British publishers declined – far from it. In 2013 a survey reported that 184,000 new and revised titles were published, putting British publishers amongst the top three most prolific in the world per million inhabitants.

What changed for the British book printer was *how and where* the books were manufactured. The exodus to overseas, lower cost markets accelerated, led by colour books and then other book work where a lead time of four to five weeks for delivery could be built into publishing schedules.

The main overseas competitors were Italy, Spain and Portugal, Holland and Belgium, Hungary and East Germany, India and the Far East (China, Hong Kong)

Work required quickly (within a month) remained in the UK, including paperbacks serviced by the few specialist A- and B-format web offset printers.

Long established UK traditional book printing companies ran into trouble and a number closed. Many senior sales staff, well connected with the London publishers, became sales agents for overseas companies making liaison between the publisher and the overseas supplier straightforward and convenient.

By the 1990s digital production services for bookwork were developing. Digital offered the advantage of short run, low cost production initially of mono books at 50 to 500 copies. Publishers could use this approach for market testing

and self-publishing individuals using PC-based desktop publishing systems could conveniently produce short editions. By 2010 digital services could produce from one copy upwards and rapidly reprint more when required.

By 2013, 60,000 of the 184,000 titles published were produced as digital only, representing a large increase in number of titles published but a decrease in the copies per title for an increasingly diverse readership.

The e-book market developed at the expense of printed copies. E-books represented 22% of self-published titles. However, this market may have peaked as by 2015 a decline of some 2% annually had set in.

There still remains a preference for the printed page. In the UK an average of one person per thousand still reads a book once a year. Some people read three to five printed titles per year including illustrated children's books.

Overall, book readership has declined significantly over levels seen in earlier years.

In the USA the decline in book readership is dramatic. A 2003 survey revealed:

- One third of high school graduates rarely read another book after finishing their education
- 42% of college graduates never read another printed book after graduating
- 80% of families did not buy or read a book in the previous year
- 70% of US adults have not been in a bookshop in recent years
- 57% of purchased books are not read to completion.

English remains the language of communication, education, science and research throughout the world. However, history shows that trends which start in America often follow here.

Glass's Guide

This is one of the principal price guides to the motor trade dealers for used vehicles. This guide is a good example of the evolution of printed guides and directories to fully digital 'online' only publication.

Issue no.925 of August 2016 of 1,727 pages A6 format on 29 gsm lightweight paper was the last issue printed by Wheatons under a contract which commenced in 2006.

The original monthly print run for several editions in 2006 was some 21,000 copies. By 2016 the run had reduced to 2,800 copies before print production ceased and the guide switched to digital-only, enabling users to search prices online from anywhere.

The same trend gathered pace with other trade publications which had been mainstream products at Wheatons.

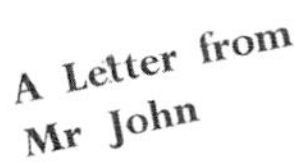

143

ONE FOUR THREE

The Quarterly Newsletter of A. Wheaton & Co. Ltd

VOL. II. NUMBER FOUR
OCT. TO DEC. 1965

A Letter from Mr John

Christmas is now almost with us and I am sure that everyone is looking forward to the few days' break.

The Christmas holiday in particular inevitably means that some people have to work at rather higher pressure than usual, not only at High Street, where the shop becomes very crowded at this time of the year, but also at the factory where a considerable amount of overtime has had to be worked in some departments in order that our deadline delivery dates can be met.

At the factory it is not only at Christmas that this need occurs and I would like to take this opportunity of thanking all members of the staff who often are asked to work long hours to help us out of our diffi-... Customers can be very insistent ... deliveries these days and we ...

143

ONE FOUR THREE

The Quarterly Newsletter of A. Wheaton & Co. Ltd

VOL. III. NUMBER TWO
APRIL TO AUGUST 1966

A Message from Mr Anthony

Our association with Pergamon is now settling down very nicely. Obviously things take time and even now there are parts of the firm where the effect of our merger has hardly been felt.

Frequent interchanges of visits are taking place between members of both companies. Mr Maxwell or Mr Buckley, both of whom are now directors of this Company, visit us every month to attend our Board Meetings. Mr John, now a director of Pergamon, attends Pergamon's Board Meetings in London. Mr Dwerryhouse and myself attend monthly meetings in Oxford to discuss production matters and the build-up of Pergamon work at Exeter. Many of Pergamon's production staff have visited us to discuss the best ways of making use of each other's capacities and abilities.

The volume of Pergamon bookwork is now

[Continued on next page.]

143

ONE FOUR THREE

The Quarterly Newsletter of A. Wheaton & Co. Ltd

VOL. II. NUMBER TWO
APRIL TO JUNE 1965

A Message from Mr John

With exports so much in the news these days it is gratifying to know that here at Wheatons we are making our fair contribution.

More than one-third of the books we publish ourselves under our own imprint are now going overseas and of those we print and bind for other publishers quite a worthwhile proportion also find their way to foreign buyers.

Apart from those members of the firm who are actually working on the export material there are many others whose work contributes indirectly so we can all feel some satisfaction with what is being done.

There are not many firms in Exeter today who are doing very much export trade and of those that do, I am sure there are very few who could match our figures.

Let us hope we can keep it up.

1964

143

ONE FOUR THREE

The Quarterly Newsletter of A. Wheaton & Co. Ltd

VOL. I. NUMBER ONE
JUNE TO SEPTEMBER

A Letter from Mr Anthony

This is the first edition of the Newsletter. The main aim of this publication is to circulate Sports Club news and activities to all members of the firm. It is a new venture, which it is hoped will help to keep everyone fully up-to-date with the Club's affairs and forthcoming events. It is also hoped to stimulate interest in the Club, amongst those who are not yet members.

The Newsletter will prove invaluable in publicizing events and conveying interesting information to readers. Although starting small, it may become larger as time goes on, as it is hoped to include several regular features. It is produced voluntarily by off-duty personnel on the firm's plant, the materials being supplied by the firm.

My only reservation is that with the interests of the firm in mind, I hope that it does not eventually grow too grand in style, incorporating full-colour half-tone illustrations, printed on art paper, case bound, with blocked case and jacketed!

A. Wheaton
Works Manager

The 143 quarterly company newsletter published with contributions from employees and news of the Sports & Social Club's activities.

Wheatons' Sports & Social Club

The club played an important part over the years in giving the company staff a focus and venue for social activities leading to comradeship and friendships which would continue for many years. A number of employees met their wives and husbands to be through being members of the club.

By 1947 the company was settling down just two years after the end of World War II. The origins of the club can be traced to 20 members who started a men-only group sharing premises with Friernhay Football Club for a subscription of one penny per week. Ladies were invited to the Christmas dinner.

The members would have puffed on their Woodbines, quaffed their ale and talked of many things – war stories included, no doubt. An important member of the group was Cyril Steer who joined the company at about this time. He had been a tool maker (precision lathe operator) at an engineering company in the Midlands.

Some of the male members group went on to found the club at 143 Fore Street after 1955. These active enthusiasts were joined by others including Cyril Steer, Bill Court, Dick Williams, John Barker, Norman Anderson, Alf Petherick and Brian Coleman.

The company made available an empty roof loft area, previously used as a paint store, above the litho plate making and camera room. Located in a side building to the main factory, the club was accessed by an exterior metal staircase at the top of a narrow alleyway from Fore Street hill.

The founder members, with a contribution from the company, fitted the premises out themselves including building the bar. Early activities included snooker, cricket, darts, a rifle section, weekly draws, table tennis and even a keep fit class. Early links were formed with other clubs in the city.

A snooker table was bought by Cyril Steer and Brian Coleman from the Civil Service Club in Heavitree, for £42 including cues, rests, balls and the surrounding wood floor. Soon a piano and a single speaker record player were acquired.

Within the first few years the club committee ran into financial difficulties not entirely of their own making but through embezzlement of funds – the club ran into losses. A new chairman, secretary and committee were elected and began the task of putting the club's finances on a firm footing.

Continued on page 142

The oldest swinger in town . . .

We now have a "Club House" to be proud of, and an assortment of functions and facilities unequalled by many other Clubs in the district. So take advantage of the sponsorships, etc. that you as Club members can enjoy. Keep your eyes on the notice boards (there's plenty of "Coming Events notified already).

"Our Gang"

October 6th	*Club Cabaret Night*
October 13th	*Blackpool Illuminations*
October 21st	*Motor Show* (£2.50 entry)
October 27th	*Hen Party*
November 1st	*Bridgewater Carnival*
November 3rd	*Bonfire Night*
December 15th	*Birmingham Shopping Trip*
December 21st	*Christmas Skittles*
December 22nd	*Christmas Dinner Dance*
December 31st	*New Year's Eve Party*

IN THE CLUB
Putting on weight at the moment are Sue Thorne, "Dolly" Wills and Tracy (Roberts) Kingdom.
(Yours truly offers his services to any other girls who may feel the need)

ANOTHER WILLIAMS
Wendy Pollard became Mrs Williams in August

IN A "BICKLE"
Congratulations to Gill Warman on marrying her Fred on 8th September

Some unanswered Questions

Did Jackie stamp on Keith's foot and give Barbara pain?
Was Frank right to have Tom done?
Did Lorraine cook, or did Kenny bake 'er?
Is Hillary's inlaws outlaws?
If Sue drew would Ken skin 'er?
Can Joe burn if Percy can?
With Charley's ball and Les's cocks would it give Trudy bliss?
Was Trevor cross when Tina phoned?
Why did he want that cloth?

FIRST CORRECT ANSWER WILL RECEIVE A BOTTLE OF WINE ON OCTOBER 6th

in the club

with contributions from **ONE FOUR THREE**

Ten years ago, in the Autumn of 1974, the Wheaton Sports & Social Club moved to the premises it now occupies, after 20 years of "Fore Street" — a place that holds fond memories for some of our older members; a place where licencing hours did not always apply; and where pre- and extra-marital "relationships" took place from time-to-time.

But the Wheaton S. & S. C. started even before this. In 1947 a "men only" membership of 20, paying 1 old penny per week, shared premises with the Friernhay Football Club. Here they played billiards, drank draught beer, smoked their Woodbines, and talked about the exploits of the "Grecians". Ladies were invited to the Christmas Dinner.

In 1955, a hard-core of members — amongst whom were Cyril Steer, Bill Court, Dick Williams, John Barker, Norman Anderson, Alf Petherick, and the "infamous" Brian Coleman, with the help of "Mr John" — went to work to convert an old paint store and other store rooms into one of the best-loved Clubs in Exeter.

Bill Court (along with George Pope and Fred Lee — both now deceased) with immaculate care and attention to detail (for which he is renowned) slapped up a few rolls of wallpaper (at 2/11d per roll, no expense was spared).

Dick Williams (then as now, always ready to cover-up things) painted the "dust" on the woodwork. Cyril did the plumbing and electrics, while John Barker and Alf Petherick (both dab hands with a hammer and saw) built the bar.

By now ladies were allowed on the membership, and the "feminine touch" was added by Doreen Marshall (now Mrs Peter Ferry) who made the curtains; and Doreen Anderson (now Mrs Peter Tothill) who covered the "sofa".

All that was missing was a snooker table; so with £42 in their pockets, Cyril Steer and Brian Coleman went "shopping" at the Civil Service Club in Heavitree and bought a table (the same one we use now), cues, rests, balls and even the wooden floor surround.

Later-on a portable skittle alley was built and installed. Players had to throw from the snooker room as the alley was too long. And it folded up against the wall when discos took place (the disco equipment being a single speaker record-player beind the bar).

An added attraction was installed in 1964 —

Cyril Steer has been successful in securing a piano which was conveyed to the Club premises by a band of willing helpers.

and to ensure things were done properly —

'cash till' register has been purchased in order to record bar takings. The firm has donated £5 towards the cost, leaving only £4 to be found by the Club.

By this time things were really moving. A "canteen" was incorporated —

I think you will agree that the tea and cakes system is now providing a good service and a good selection of cakes at reasonable prices are obtainable.
It is regretted that it will be necessary to raise the cost of tea by 6d. per week, in order to keep pace with rising costs.

and funds were building-up —

ON THE HOUSE

The Committee are pleased to announce that every member of the Sports Club will be entitled to one drink "on the house" over the Christmas period.

Snooker was a great attraction, and some budding "Joe Davises" (who) were to be found amongst the membership —

Dogherty in but Napper shock
It was with great joy that the snooker teams heard that David Dogherty had been selected to play for Exeter Under 21. But it came as a shock to find Keith Napper named only as a reserve for the match against Exmouth Under 21.

and Table Tennis too was very popular —

The table tennis tournament organised by Keith Richards was a great success. This game has become very popular, so next year we hope to see a lot more members entering. This year's winner was Len Middleton, who defeated Keith Napper three games to one.

(1965 was not a very good year for "Keef")

The newsletter continued up to the move to Marsh Barton and then became the Sports Club's news-sheet.

Darts, treasure hunts, and even a rifle club were all part of the Club Calendar, and who would dispute that Wheatons had a football team to be feared —

Same colour as Liverpool if nothing else

(no Richards or Bothams amongst this lot)

The highlight of the year was of course the "Annual Presentation of Trophies" —

(I like the hair-style and mini-skirt)

Where are they now . . .

closely followed by the Club Outing —

The boys stop for a break

And, of course, romance blossomed —

David and Myrtle

Well, that was more than 10 years ago, and on October 6th we'll be celebrating the anniversary of our existing Club as we know it now.

There used to be a saying amongst people at Fore Street, that "things will get better when we move to Marsh Barton". Well, I think from the Club's point-of-view, they certainly have. We have now totally finished the redecoration, and the girls can now "powder their noses in surroundings befitting their sex".

From this . . .

to this . . .

in just over 12 months.

On October 6th we'll have cabaret with *JETHRO*, and a *"1970's Happy Hour"* when the following prices will be charged —

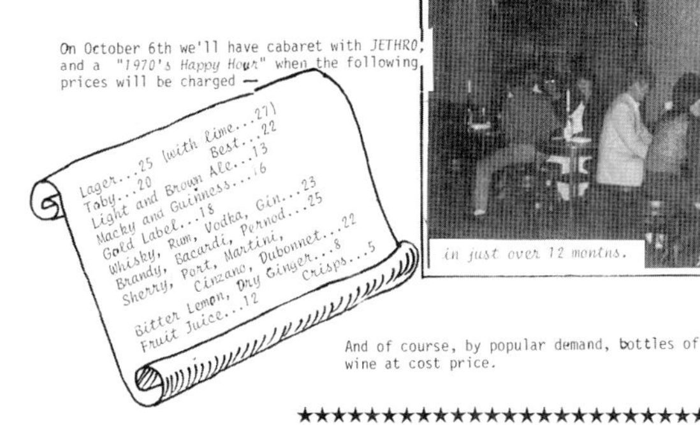

Lager...25 (with lime...27)
Toby...20 Best...22
Light and Brown Ale...13
Macky and Guinness...16
Gold Label...18
Whisky, Rum, Vodka, Gin...23
Brandy, Bacardi, Pernod...25
Sherry, Port, Martini, Cinzano, Dubonnet...22
Bitter Lemon, Dry Ginger...8
Fruit Juice...12 Crisps...5

And of course, by popular demand, bottles of wine at cost price.

★★★★★★★★★★★★★★★★★★★★★★★★★★★★★

By-and-large, the Wheaton S. & S.C. is much the same as it was in the 60's and 70's, but as times have changed, so in many ways has our Club.

Darts, snooker and skittles are still enjoyed, but table tennis has been replaced by pool. The record player and piano have been replaced by stereophonic sound and flashing lights and a juke-box; and carpet-tiles and woodblock have taken over from lino-covered floors. Day trips by "charabanc" to Plymouth are now replaced by weekends in Belgium.

But I am sure that many members would still like to stagger down the iron staircase to the unlit toilets before going home a 2 a.m. on a Saturday morning.

Times change and life-styles change, but people remain the same, and none more-so than our members. We still have the "hard-core" organising and running things; we still have the girls coming to the dances to let their hair down (but not their knickers now); and we still have members who are "hard to please"

And, as always, we still have people who give time and effort for the benefit of others.

The "King Wallys" Knock-out team

With one event still to go (another Assault Course) so far this year Wheatons members have amassed in excess of £2000 for various charities (and some years ago we had to borrow £5 from the Company to buy a "cash register").

Continued from page 139

The June 1964 minutes recorded new officers shown below.

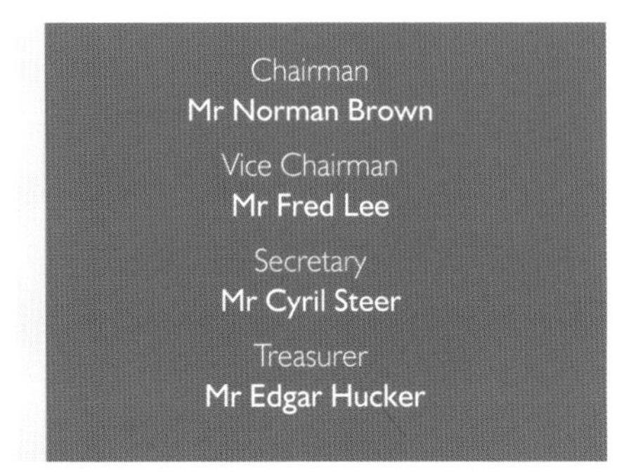
Chairman
Mr Norman Brown
Vice Chairman
Mr Fred Lee
Secretary
Mr Cyril Steer
Treasurer
Mr Edgar Hucker

By September 1964 the club had 104 members.

Within a year these officers and their committee had restored the club's finances, paid off creditors and were making monthly profits.

The Chairman, Mr Brown, was the Letterpress Department foreman. He had moved down to Wheatons from Newcastle. He was a north countryman who brought a firm organising style to his department and was a great help to the club at this time.

In 1964 the company commenced publishing a quarterly house journal – *143*. This publication continued until the club moved to Marsh Barton in the autumn of 1974. The club's activities, the officers and committees were recorded in copies of the earlier editions which still survive from 1964, 1965 and 1966.

By 1974 the club moved to purpose built premises at the front of the new factory at Marsh Barton. The premises now included a function room and bar, kitchen, snooker room, toilet facilities and a portable skittle alley.

The *143* house Journal became the newsletter of the club and was published from time to time.

At Marsh Barton the club blossomed, much helped by the availability of car parking for members, associate members and guests. Over a period of 15 years at the new premises the club became one of the most vibrant in Exeter, not only through its own activities but by associations with other local clubs.

An amusing Robert Maxwell incident that took place in the mid-1980s was recalled by Peter Webber (Assistant Secretary). At the end of one of Maxwell's visits to the company Peter recalls, 'I opened the Club at 7 p.m. and his olive green Rolls Royce and Claud his driver were waiting in the rain outside the main door. I offered Claude inside and a drink whilst waiting which he accepted. At about 8 p.m. Mr Maxwell (and others which I cannot recall) came into the club and said

to me (I had met him two or three times previously) "Come on Webber, show me this club I'm paying for". I proceeded to show him around and went into the snooker room. There was a local match in progress with one of the away team's players about to take a very easy shot on a red ball. Mr Maxwell put his hand on the table between the cue ball and the red saying "And what do you do?" mistaking him for an employee. This gentleman, not knowing who Mr Maxwell was, and thinking he said "And what are you going to do", stated "I'm going to pot that red if you take your f***ing hand off the table". Mr Maxwell replied "I'll bet 20 pence you don't, Claud put 20 p on the table". The gentleman took his shot and missed. Mr Maxwell pocketed the two 20 p pieces and we resumed our 'tour'. Once back in the main bar Mr Maxwell instructed Claude to put £20 on the bar and buy everybody a drink "including that loser in there" pointing to the snooker room. On his way out I said to Mr Maxwell, "Fancy taking that chap's 20 p," to which he replied, "I'm a gambler Webber, be it 20 p or 20 million, if I win I take the spoils".

By 1989 practically every employee of the company was a member of the club. The subscription was 2 p per week and this was deducted from salary at source. There were also approximately 140 Associate Members who paid a £1.50 annual membership fee. There were many family members and friends of members who took part in the various activities such as skittles, snooker, darts, and table tennis, and a few members who were in the club's football team. Many members used the club for functions including wedding receptions, birthdays, anniversaries and retirement parties which were always thoroughly enjoyed due to the low cost of the bar drinks.

The Wheatons' football team provided players to make up the team of the GPMU union. They played away games against the teams of other book printers and paper mills.

By virtue of the low cost of the bar drinks, many people requested Associate Membership but rules restricted the club to a limit of 20% of full membership numbers. The price of bar drinks was in the lowest three of clubs in the city due mainly to the fact that the company only charged the club £5 per annum notional rent and made no charge for utilities.

During Peter Webber's 16 years as Assistant Secretary, Chairman and Secretary, thousands of pounds were raised for various charities, amongst which were Franklin Hospital, Mother and Baby Unit, the CLIC Sargent and the Stroke Unit at the Royal Devon and Exeter (RD&E) Hospital. The monies were raised by members partaking in 12-hour skittles, 12-hour darts, 12-hour disco dancing and indoor and outdoor Superstars. All these events took place in the club apart from the outdoor Superstars which took place in the grounds of St Thomas's High School. Participants had a choice of any six from eight events. On one occasion only one member chose long distance running from the club to the Double Locks and back, which Peter Webber made him do whilst accompanying him on a bicycle.

In the 1990s, due to the reorganisation of the company involving accommodating Techset within the Sports & Social Club premises, the club had to find new premises, which were found in the old Labour Club in Clifton Hill. Unfortunately, although having a skittle alley and main bar there was no room for a snooker table or any functions. The club had to hire the main function room from the Labour Party and along with the cost of rent and utilities the club began incurring losses. The majority of members continued their membership for the first two or three years but gradually ceased their membership due to the inconvenience, lack of parking facilities and increasing prices. The loss of full members meant that the club's Associate Members' numbers were in jeopardy. In 1993 Peter Webber and his wife Pamela called an Extraordinary General Meeting to propose converting to a Proprietary Members Club which was accepted. The club continued to run under this banner for the next two years but the full time work commitments of Peter Webber and his wife meant they finally had to 'call it a day' in December 1995.

History must record the dedication of the club's committed stalwarts who, over the years, gave so much of their own time to the club's affairs. They were the officers, committee members, organisers of the sports and social events and often their wives. All these people and others made Wheatons' Sports & Social Club such a success.

Written by Anthony Wheaton with main contributions from Peter Webber

Printer's Pie

Introduction

The term 'printer's pie' originates from the early days of typesetting when all text composition used Founders type and individual sorts (characters), setting by hand. If the compositor's hand slipped, the type became a mess or 'pied'. Over the years, 'printer's pie' became a general term for a jumble or mixture of things to do with the printing industry. Similarly to processes in other manufacturing industries, over just the past 50 years printing industry processes have been computerised, digitised and automated. This has resulted in the loss of the old trades and the skilled employment of thousands and thousands of journeymen along with the work and social comradeship they enjoyed.

The old letterpress and litho trade procedures and practices survive in a few very small private print shops but in the wider industry will never be seen again.

This section, called Printer's Pie is a snapshot of the trades and practices which were fundamental to Wheatons' history in Exeter, beginning with the issue of safety.

Safety

Before the advent of UK health and safety legislation and improved guarding of machinery, printing and typesetting could be dangerous trades. One distraction, or a printer instinctively grabbing a crumpled sheet, could lead to a crushed hand in a clam shell platen printing press or in the delivery of a printing machine.

The blankets and plate cylinders on litho presses were washed up by hand. The printer's assistant had shrouded control buttons on each printing unit so that he could advance the cylinder around in small movements. The practice was known as 'inching'. However, if he dwelt too long on the button the cylinders could rotate further than intended, pick up his cleaning cloth and pull the cloth and perhaps fingers into the in-running nip. Many printers and assistants would have experienced nips or worse before the advent of the 'true inch' system in the 1970s. The true inch system limited the movement of the cylinders to small increments before stopping.

Bindery staff had to be careful to avoid catching their hair in the revolving chuck spindles of paper drilling machines which could risk a torn scalp. The early buckle folding machines were extremely noisy before noise muffling hoods were added on later models.

Compositors worked all day handling lead type. Monotype type casters were the noisiest machines, probably exceeding 100 decibels at a time when ear defenders were not in common use. Also, there were the fumes from the molten lead type metal pots.

Before the advent of safety shoes, handling a 32-page letterpress form of type in the order of 190 kilos could be a risky business. When lifting a form into the printing press one slip could lead to broken toes or badly pinched fingers.

On Intertype typesetting machines, if the mould wheel had not located accurately to fit in contact with the type metal injection nozzle, there would be a 'splash'. This resulted in metal at 260°C squirting out over the face of the mould wheel and beyond. If fragments of molten metal reached the arm of the nearby operator there would be deep burns.

Exposed film from gallery cameras was hand developed and fixed in large shallow trays. One tray containing cyanide was stored in the camera room. Operators had to be respectful of their chemicals. If the red light was on above the camera room door one stayed away.

In the 1960s, printing was rated the third most dangerous trade after mining and commercial fishing.

Typesetting

By 1440 Johann Guttenberg had invented movable type consisting of individual carved boxwood letters to compose words for letterpress printing.

He progressed to having type letters cast in metal in foundries. The cast type became known as Founders type which, for the smaller type sizes, could be purchased by typesetters in complete typefaces. Large type for posters continued in wood.

Early Wheatons' compositors set up type in compositors' 'sticks' (a hand held narrow tray with a fixed end and side lip and a sliding wedge). Individual type 'sorts': characters, spaces, punctuation and numerals, were all contained in wooden trays, or 'cases', comprising some 112 small compartments to accommodate one size of type. Each size of type was accommodated in a separate case. All cases under one compositor's frame would represent a complete typeface range, e.g. for Baskerville. Cases of type were mounted on slide rails under 'composing frames'. The top of the frame was angled at 25 and 45 degrees so that a compositor could mount a case of type on the frame to pick type for hand composition in his stick. Once several lines were assembled the type would be lifted out onto a 'galley'. This was a three-sided tray approximately 24 inches long and 6 or 8 inches wide with a stop end. As lines of type were set and lifted onto the galley, they built up pages which were then space divided and folioed before the commencement of the next. A galley would contain three pages of set type locked up by a side 'reglet' (wood strip) and wedges to hold the pages secure.

A typesetting composing stick

A tray of wooden type blocks

There was no tobacco smoking in Composing Rooms, the usual stimulant was snuff snorted from the forearm.

A sort (a single letter) cast from type metal on its body

The Composing Room at Fore Street during the 1920s. Compositors can be seen typesetting by hand from cased type characters. To the right 'stonehands' are imposing type pages in steel chases known as 'forms' for printing.

Note the Columbian Press in the background (top right).

Galleys with type were then inked and proofed to paper on a galley press. The proofs, known as 'galley proofs', were read by readers to check for any corrections. If corrections were required they would be undertaken by the compositor working from readers' 'marks' in the margins and in the text. The galley would then be proofed again. Once any 'revised' corrections were checked, approved pages were tied around by thin cord to keep the type compacted. If type was upset or knocked it became 'off its feet' and was referred to as being 'pied' if lines fell over and characters were disturbed.

Readers' marks were a set of symbols used by readers and editors to instruct compositors.

Once all the pages of a book had been set, proofed and corrected on galleys, proofs would be signed off by the readers. Galleys were stored in racks to await 'imposition'.

Imposition was the process of laying out type pages on a precision flat table like cast iron 'stone' about 8 by 5 feet in size. Individual pages were slid off the galleys in required folio order to be positioned on the stone to folding layouts in multiples of 8 or 16 pages, i.e. 8 pages, 16 pages, 32 pages, etc. A steel frame known as a 'chase' was then laid over to contain the pages. The retaining strings around the pages were then removed. Spacers (known as 'furniture') were added in required margins, head and foot areas. The type and furniture assembly were then locked up in the chase by key operated mechanical expanding wedges (coins). The form was then checked for lift to ensure that no type dropped on lifting. Large heavy 32-page impositions would require steel locking bracing bars to be added inside

B.S. 1219 : 1945

SYMBOLS FOR CORRECTING PROOFS

possible all corrections should be made in the margin ; only such ng made in the text as are required to indicate the place to which ction refers.
three or more corrections occur in one line, the corrections should d between the left and right margins, the order being always from ight.
n an alteration is desired in a letter, word or words, the existing tc., should be struck through and the letter or matter to be substi- hould be written in the margin, followed by /.
ords printed in italics in the marginal mark column below are in- ons and not part of the marks.)

No.	Marginal mark	Meaning	Corresponding mark in text
	/	Sign to show that marginal mark is concluded	
	δ/	Delete (take out)	/
	δ/	Delete and close-up	/ above and below letters to be taken out.
4	#	Delete and leave space	/
5	*stet*	Leave as printed	.... under letters or words to remain.
6	*caps*	Change to capital letters	≡ under letters or words to be altered.
7	*s.c.*	Change to small capitals	= under letters or words to be altered.
8	*caps & s.c.*	Use capital letters for initial letters and small capitals for rest of words	≡ under initial letters and = under the rest of the words
9	*l.c.*	Change to lower case	Encircle letters to be altered.
10	*bold* or *clar*	Change to bold type	~~~ under letters or words to be altered.

Page 50

No.	Marginal mark	Meaning	Corresponding mark in text
11	*ital*	Change to italics	—— under letters or words to be altered.
12	*insert rule*	Underline word or words	—— under words affected.
13	*rom*	Change to roman type	Encircle words to be altered.
14	*w.f.*	(wrong fount) Replace by letter of correct fount	Encircle letter to be altered.
15	9	Invert type	Encircle letter to be altered.
16	×	Replace by similar but undamaged character	Encircle letter to be altered.
17	7	Substituted letters or signs under which this is placed to be 'superior'	Encircle letters or signs to be altered.
18	7	Inserted letters or signs under which this is placed to be 'superior'	⋏
19	7	Substituted letters or signs over which this is placed to be 'inferior'	Encircle letters or signs to be altered.
20	7	Inserted letters or signs over which this is placed to be 'inferior'	⋏
21	⁀ ‿ *Enclosing ligature or diphthong required*	Use ligature (e.g., ﬃ) or diphthong (e.g., œ)	⁀ ‿ enclosing letters to be altered.
22	*Write out separate letters followed by* /	Substitute separate letters for ligature or diphthong	/ through ligature or diphthong to be altered.
23	⁀ ‿	Close-up—delete space between letters	⁀ ‿ linking words or letters.
24	#	Insert space	⋏
25	# >	Space between lines or paragraphs*	
26	*eq* #	Make spacing equal	∟ between words.

*Amount of space may be indicated.

Page 51

Wheaton's provided editors with this booklet containing the Wheaton 'editorial house style' which was specific to company requirements. This booklet also contained a copy of the British Standard No 1219 1945 proof reading marks. These synmbols were the industry standard for proof readers and editors alike.

the form to avoid springing. Forms were then stored in form racks, in order, making up the pagination of a book prior to letterpress printing.

After printing an edition, many publishers, including Pergamon, required the type to be held in storage pending reprints. For this service the company would charge 'type rent'. Stored type represented a considerable tied up investment for the printer.

Standing type with an early prospect of reuse was stored in cabinet racks on galleys. For longer term storage, pages would be wrapped in newspaper and stored several pages high on shelving.

When the Pergamon major typesetting programme built up in the 1960s there was insufficient storage space remaining for standing type. Cabinets were obtained from the printers' sundry supplies company, Cornerstone, but the units were expensive.

Anthony Wheaton came up with a design for a high density storage solution at a third of the cost of conventional racks. The system involved overhead angle iron gantry frames about 10 feet long, 6 feet high and the depth of a galley. Every 4 feet steel legs supported the overhead frame. Steel sheets hung from

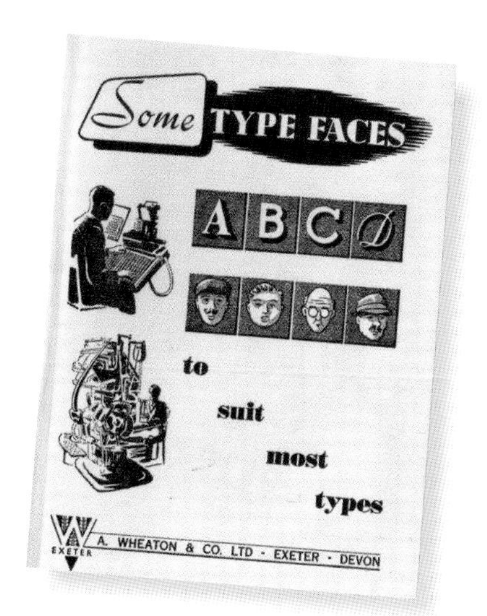

An early Wheaton typestyle catalogue

the gantry with a lip back and front for stability. The sheets were spaced apart, just wider than a galley and were drilled with holes just bigger than three-eighths of an inch. The holes were arranged in rows of four horizontally and 3 inches apart vertically from the top to the bottom near the floor. Three-eighths of an inch steel rods were run through all of the holes representing the length of the rack. Galleys with stored type were slid onto the four bars.

Hundreds of lower cost galleys were manufactured by Brown & Co, Commercial Road. A number of racks were assembled by the company's Engineering and Maintenance team, Cyril Steer, Alf Petherick and John Barker, to hold thousands of pages.

Prior to printing, some publishers required Wheatons' 'book proof' service. Book proofs were produced in small quantities of ten or 20 and printed by composing room stonehand, Bob Brereton, using a flatbed proofing press large enough to take imposed forms of type. Hand folded sheets were bound with a pull over soft cover. The book proofs were used by publishers as advance copies for reviews and initial publicity.

A Monotype type caster as installed at Wheatons from 1935

All typesetting at Wheatons was hand set from case up until the 1930s, and continued to be in part until 1965. Monotype mechanical typesetting was first introduced at Fore Street in 1935.

Founders type held in case for hand setting at Fore Street amounted to 18 typefaces for 6pt (point) to 12pt for text and 36pt to 48pt for headlines. Monotype and Intertype faces for mechanical typesetting covered nine typefaces for 6pt to 14pt for text.

After use, Founders type was scrubbed off with turpentine and 'dissed' to redistribute every individual character back into case by hand for reuse.

Mechanical type was melted down and cast in moulds to ingots for reuse. Type metal for mechanical typesetting was an alloy of 74% lead, 10% tin and 16% antimony. The molten working temperature of type metal for Monotype casting was 286° C. Metal set at 240°C.

Founders type contained less lead and was a harder alloy enabling longer use of the handset type with reduced wear.

Every individual type character was cast on its body to a height of 0.918 inch – known as 'type high'. In type sizes, 72 points = 1 inch. The standard unit of measure for type bodies was 12 points = 1 'pica'. Lines of type were measured in picas. Each type size had its own body size and for the widest letter this was known as an 'em', i.e. 6 point ems, 8 point ems, etc. If no em was referred to in a type description, the default was the 12 point em.

Bodies were just shoulder height on the 'sort' (type character). Widths of spaces were described as ems, ens (half an em) also known as 'muttons' and 'nuts' respectively. Spacers below an en were thicks, middles and thins. Then there were leads (rules) for bodying out between paragraphs, etc. as 2 pt, 3 pt, 4 pt, etc. Leads were cut to just under line length by the compositor in his 'lead cutter'.

By 1935 Wheatons had installed their first Monotype keyboards and type casters followed by two Intertype machines (similar to Linotypes favoured by newspaper publishers).

The Monotype hot metal typesetting system became widely used in the trade. Monotype went on to design a well respected range of typefaces many of which were added at Wheatons for publishers' quality work.

The Monotype system involved a keyboard with alphabetical characters, accents, punctuation, numerals, etc. displayed on individual keys.

The keyboard operator keyed from manuscript copy. Each key pneumatically punched a hole in an advancing paper tape roll. Experienced operators could read the tape code and could correct keying errors by applying pasted paper patches.

The punched paper tape was 'read' by the type casting machine by pneumatic pins which felt out the hole positions to cast the required letters in metal type. Also on the keyboard was a drum scale, relevant to each point size of type, which would show the keyboard operator the spacing required to 'justify' the line of type (fill out between the words to required pica 'measure'). This information was also punched into the tape. When the caster operator loaded the punched spool on the caster, the spool was turned over so that the casting machine first read the settings for the justification spacing for each line.

Each character was cast in a mould from the chosen typeface as a matrix, one letter at a time. As each line built up it was automatically advanced onto a type galley

A printer's pica rule

to build up a continuous length of page type. The type matrixes were contained in a 'die case' of 15 x 15 and later 15 x 17 character layouts. At the commencement of a job the caster operator set up the die case with the required characters. Individual matrixes were contained in the die cases by rods from one side to the other.

Wheatons' first move into technical typesetting involved the installation of one Monotype 'D' keyboard. The 'D' keyboard was larger than the typesetting keyboard and displayed on keys the additional characters for mathematical composition. This keyboard remained in use after the move to Marsh Barton and enabled the company to commence typesetting more complex technical text for Pergamon Press.

Experienced keyboard operator, Peter Tothill, could play the keyboard like an organ. On one occasion when Russian visitors were having a tour of the Composing Room, they were given a demonstration – their eyes became glazed but it was noticed that they had seen the pin ups on Peter's wall!

The Monotype equipment at Fore Street finally built up to six keyboards and four to five casters including one lead and rule caster.

Type metal ingots were fed into the electric melting pots on the casters, suspended by an overhead chain. Ingots automatically lowered into the melting pot as the metal was used. The surface of the molten type metal was skimmed off periodically to remove 'dross', as impurities would otherwise build up and choke the casting nozzles.

The maestro on the casters, working double shifts by 1965, was the most energetic Ern Litton who, in spite of the shattering noise, would run three composition casters at a time (when only two were required) to easily earn himself a 167 bonus level each week. He soon had his Triumph 2000!

The Intertype process worked from an integrated keyboard and casting machine. The keys released matrixes from an overhead magazine. As the operator keyed from copy, the matrixes slid down tracks and built up as a line in an 'assembler'. When the line was 'sent away' to the casting wheel, molten type metal cast a complete line of type as a 'slug'. The mould was water cooled. The slugs were assembled on a galley to make up columns of type. After casting, the matrixes returned to the magazine via a top 'dissing' screw rail, ready to be selected again. Each magazine held a specific typeface. Intertype typesetting was favoured for lower quality work as the typefaces were not quite so well defined as in Monotype. An advantage was that the slugs were easy to handle for page make up and locked up securely in a chase. Slugs could not be 'pied'.

By 1965 the first film-setting systems were becoming available to the printing trade. Initially, both the Monotype Corporation and the Linotype company (similar to Intertype) developed equipment based on their hot metal equivalent. These systems incorporated photo matrixes into metal matrix bodies. Wheatons allowed time for the new approach to typesetting to develop further before investing.

By the 1970s, Monotype came out with the Lasercomp and Linotype with the Linotron 505 in association with K S Paul & Co.

In 1972 Wheatons' first move into computer typesetting and film setting began with the purchase of a Comprite Company 'front end' system linked to a Monotype Lasercomp typesetter. Technical text could be produced on this equipment with prior encoding. The system was upgraded with increased computing power and magnetic tape storage in 1973 to 1974.

Laser typesetting involved digitising the master type font characters to a resolution of 1,000 lines per inch. Digitised typefaces were purchased from the Monotype Corporation either as single faces or in bundles supplied on computer discs.

Wheatons' Lasercomps were loaded with the principal typefaces favoured by book publishers at the time. These were Baskerville, Century, Nimrod, Photina, Bembo, Ehrhardt, Palatino, Plantin and Times New Roman including the full range of mathematical Pi fonts.

Computer typesetting progressed in stages. The Comprite system had no page make up programme. Initial output from the Lasercomp was to bromide photographic paper.

Pages were made up and finalised with running heads, folios and illustrations by page make up compositors. Make up was undertaken on inclined work benches similar to a draftsman's. Page grids (similar to graph paper) with page format borders defined and printed in light blue were used to make up the pages by 'cut and paste'. The bromide paper was first wax coated to adhere to the grids. Pages were then Xerox proofed for reading and checking, prior to being photographed to film or used as camera-ready copy (CRC) in the Rachwal direct to plate system. The light blue background grid would not photograph to film.

Pergamon's scientific and technical journals involved increasingly complex mathematical typesetting with graphs.

By 1973 to 1974, after considerable research and development, Wheatons began working with Bedford

A. Wheaton & Co. Ltd

Computer Typesetting

The company uses the Monotype Lasercomp Mark II for the typesetting output onto film or paper. The output image is created from digitised type founts providing a character resolution of 1000 lines per inch. A comprehensive range of general book faces are available, samples of which are shown overleaf. For the more technical and complex setting of mathematics we recommend the use of the Times New Roman range of typefaces and below we show some sample alphabets and the range of ancillary founts and pi-characters currently available to provide for mathematical text and display equation typesetting.

TIMES NEW ROMAN Synopsis in 10pt

Roman Caps	ABCDEFGHIJKLMNOPQRSTUVWXYZ&ÆŒÅ
Roman Small Caps	ABCDEFGHIJKLMNOPQRSTUVWXYZ&ÆŒÅ
Roman Lower Case	abcdefghijklmnopqrstuvwxyzæœ ß fi ff fl ffi ffl (dotless) ı ȷ (alternative) ɑ g
Floating Accents	(all founts)
Roman Figures, Punctuation, Signs	1234567890$£/.,:;'‘'!?%‰ -()[]{}⟨⟩–—*†‡§¶ + − × =
Italic Caps	*ABCDEFGHIJKLMNOPQRSTUVWXYZ&ÆŒÅ*
Italic Lower Case	*abcdefghijklmnopqrstuvwxyzæœßfiffflffiffl* (dotless) *ı ȷ* (alternative) *g*
Italic Figures, Punctuation, Signs	*1234567890$£/.,:;'‘'!?%‰ -()[]{}⟨⟩–—*†‡§¶* + − × =
Bold Caps	**ABCDEFGHIJKLMNOPQRSTUVWXYZ&ÆŒÅ**
Bold Lower Case	**abcdefghijklmnopqrstuvwxyzæœßfiffflffiffl** (dotless) **ı ȷ** (alternative) **ɑg**
Bold Figures, Punctuation, Signs	**1234567890$£/.,:;'‘'!?%‰ -()[]–—*†‡§¶** + − × =
Bold Italic Caps	***ABCDEFGHIJKLMNOPQRSTUVWXYZ&ÆŒÅ***
Bold Italic Lower Case	***abcdefghijklmnopqrstuvwxyzæœßfiffflffiffl*** (dotless) ***ı ȷ*** (alternative) ***g***
Bold Italic Figures, Punctuation, Signs	***1234567890$£/.,:;'‘'!?%‰ -()[]–—*†‡§¶*** + − × =
Times Greek Roman	ϑςεερτυθιπασδφϕγηξκϰλζχψωβνμϚΥΘΕΠΣΔΦΓΞΛΨΩϒϖ
Times Greek Italic	*ϑςεερτυθιπασδφϕγηξκϰλζχψωβνμϚΥΘΕΠΣΔΦΓΞΛΨΩϒϖ*
Times Greek Bold	**ϑςεερτυθιπασδφϕγηξκϰλζχψωβνμϚΥΘΕΠΣΔΦΓΞΛΨΩϒϖ**
Times Greek Bold Italic	***ϑςεερτυθιπασδφϕγηξκϰλζχψωβνμϚΥΘΕΠΣΔΦΓΞΛΨΩϒϖ***
Times Script Medium	ABCDEFGHIJKLMNOPQRSTUVWXYZ abcdefghijklmnopqrstuvwxyz
Times Script Bold	ABCDEFGHIJKLMNOPQRSTUVWXYZ abcdefghijklmnopqrstuvwxyz
Times Fraktur Medium	𝔄𝔅ℭ𝔇𝔈𝔉𝔊ℌℑ𝔍𝔎𝔏𝔐𝔑𝔒𝔓𝔔ℜ𝔖𝔗𝔘𝔙𝔚𝔛𝔜ℨ𝔞𝔟𝔠𝔡𝔢𝔣𝔤𝔥𝔦𝔧𝔩𝔪𝔫𝔬𝔭𝔮𝔯𝔰𝔱𝔲𝔳𝔴𝔵𝔶𝔷
Times Fraktur Bold	𝕬𝕭𝕮𝕯𝕰𝕱𝕲𝕳𝕴𝕵𝕶𝕷𝕸𝕹𝕺𝕻𝕼𝕽𝕾𝕿𝖀𝖁𝖂𝖃𝖄𝖅𝖆𝖇𝖈𝖉𝖊𝖋𝖌𝖍𝖎𝖏𝖑𝖒𝖓𝖔𝖕𝖖𝖗𝖘𝖙𝖚𝖛𝖜𝖝𝖞𝖟
Open Face	ABCDEFGHIJKLMNOPQRSTUVWXYZabcdefghijklmnopqrstuvwxyz 1234567890ϑςερτυθιεπασδφγηξκλζχψωβνμϚρΥΘΕΠΣΔΦΞΛΦΩϒ
Phonetics	ɑβɔɕçɣdðɖɗʤɖʑeɘəɚɛɝɟɡɓɦħɥɧɨɫɬɮɱmɯɰnɲŋɳɵøɶoɸqʀɹɾɽɻʂʃʆʈθʧʉʊʋʌʍʎɣʏzʐʒʔʕʢʘɐɑɒɔ
Maths Pi Founts	( ) [ ] { } √ ∑ ∫ ∮ ‖ ⟨ ⟩ (etc)

< > ≤ ≥ ≦ ≧ ⋚ ⋛ ≪ ≫ ≮ ≯ ≰ ≱ ≠ ≢ ≈ ≃ ≅ ≡ ± ∓ ÷ ∴ ∵ ← → ⇌ ∪ ∩ ⊂ ⊃ ⊥ ∠ ⊆ ⊇ ≙ ∝ ∇ ⊲ ⊳ ⊴ ⊵ # ≭ ≁ ⊀ ⊁ ⇄ ⇆ ↔ ↕ ⟶ ⟵ (etc)

Typeface – Times New Roman, an example of the comprehensive range of alphabets, ancillary type founts and extraneous symbols known as Pi-characters held in 10 pt type size. This range and typeface was used by the company for scientific and academic computer typesetting.

Computer Corporation in Massachusetts, USA. Bedford had developed a 'real time' computer typesetting system for displayed financial reports. Real time working enabled the keyboard operator to see, for the first time, the result of each key depression immediately on computer screen so that he could build up complex pages and correct any errors. Bedford developed their system with Wheatons to set mathematics in real time. This approach became known as 'wysiwyg' – what you see is what you get. There was no prior encoding of text necessary.

Wheatons' installation was the first in the UK and included Bedford interactive editing terminals. Text input was from 20 keyboards supplied by Device Technology UK. The keyboard layout was based on a 'querty' word processor layout but with some 11 levels of underlying shift on the most frequently used character keys to access the wide range of special characters and symbols required for mathematical setting.

The layout was developed by experienced keyboard operators Malcolm Alden and Tony Vinnicombe who worked on the layout in a secluded room for six weeks to complete the work.

In 1983, to cope with the demands of the *Radio Times*, a second Bedford system and a second Monotype Lasercomp Mark II were added.

The Computer Typesetting Department now employed 80 staff working on double shifts. Wheatons could now set the most complex mathematics commanding a price of £20–22 per page in the market.

In 1987 the Computer Typesetting Department was restructured as Polestar Digital Techset. The Bedford system was further upgraded to a Target Vision XL system with ten Bedford intelligent editing and page make up terminals and 27 Device Technology text input terminals. One Lasercomp was upgraded to a Lasercomp Pioneer which enabled text and graphics to be output together to final film pages.

Techset later employed 85 skilled and well paid staff, with Reed Elsevier by far the largest customer. There were also some non-Group journal customers.

By 1999, and following the devastating announcement that the Reed Elsevier journals (ex-Pergamon) were to be outsourced to Indian companies at far lower prices, the department was rundown and closed. The journal typeset pages were received back over the internet from India for printing at Wheatons, so all the company had to do was impose the pages for printing.

Techset had become a casualty of advancing technology, the internet and free trade.

The Bedford intelligence editing and page make up terminal for complex typsetting

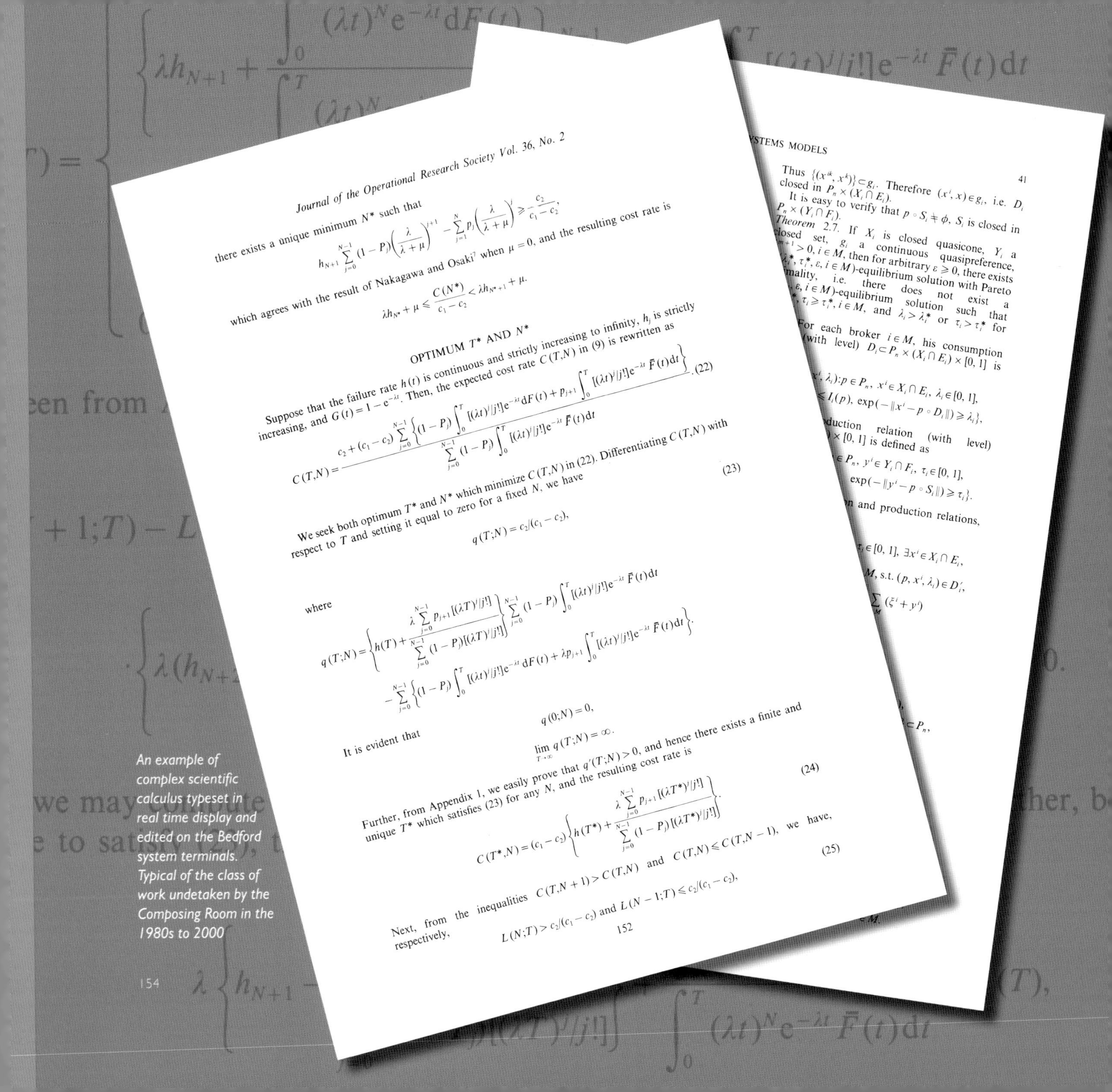
Journal of the Operational Research Society Vol. 36, No. 2

there exists a unique minimum N^* such that

$$h_{N+1}\sum_{j=0}^{N-1}(1-P_j)\left(\frac{\lambda}{\lambda+\mu}\right)^{j+1} - \sum_{j=1}^{N} p_j\left(\frac{\lambda}{\lambda+\mu}\right)^j \geqslant \frac{c_2}{c_1-c_2},$$

which agrees with the result of Nakagawa and Osaki[7] when $\mu = 0$, and the resulting cost rate is

$$\lambda h_{N^*}+\mu \leqslant \frac{C(N^*)}{c_1-c_2} < \lambda h_{N^*+1}+\mu.$$

OPTIMUM T^* AND N^*

Suppose that the failure rate $h(t)$ is continuous and strictly increasing to infinity, h_j is strictly increasing, and $G(t) = 1 - e^{-\lambda t}$. Then, the expected cost rate $C(T,N)$ in (9) is rewritten as

$$C(T,N)=\frac{c_2+(c_1-c_2)\sum_{j=0}^{N-1}\left\{(1-P_j)\int_0^T[(\lambda t)^j/j!]e^{-\lambda t}\,dF(t)+p_{j+1}\int_0^T[(\lambda t)^j/j!]e^{-\lambda t}\bar{F}(t)\,dt\right\}}{\sum_{j=0}^{N-1}(1-P_j)\int_0^T[(\lambda t)^j/j!]e^{-\lambda t}\bar{F}(t)\,dt}. \quad (22)$$

We seek both optimum T^* and N^* which minimize $C(T,N)$ in (22). Differentiating $C(T,N)$ with respect to T and setting it equal to zero for a fixed N, we have

$$q(T;N)=c_2/(c_1-c_2), \quad (23)$$

where

$$q(T;N)=\left\{h(T)+\frac{\lambda\sum_{j=0}^{N-1}p_{j+1}[(\lambda T)^j/j!]}{\sum_{j=0}^{N-1}(1-P_j)[(\lambda T)^j/j!]}\right\}\sum_{j=0}^{N-1}(1-P_j)\int_0^T[(\lambda t)^j/j!]e^{-\lambda t}\bar{F}(t)\,dt - \sum_{j=0}^{N-1}\left\{(1-P_j)\int_0^T[(\lambda t)^j/j!]e^{-\lambda t}\,dF(t)+\lambda p_{j+1}\int_0^T[(\lambda t)^j/j!]e^{-\lambda t}\bar{F}(t)\,dt\right\}.$$

It is evident that

$$q(0;N)=0,$$
$$\lim_{T\to\infty} q(T;N)=\infty.$$

Further, from Appendix 1, we easily prove that $q'(T;N)>0$, and hence there exists a finite and unique T^* which satisfies (23) for any N, and the resulting cost rate is

$$C(T^*,N)=(c_1-c_2)\left\{h(T^*)+\frac{\lambda\sum_{j=0}^{N-1}p_{j+1}[(\lambda T^*)^j/j!]}{\sum_{j=0}^{N-1}(1-P_j)[(\lambda T^*)^j/j!]}\right\}. \quad (24)$$

Next, from the inequalities $C(T,N+1)>C(T,N)$ and $C(T,N)\leqslant C(T,N-1)$, we have, respectively,

$$L(N;T)>c_2/(c_1-c_2) \text{ and } L(N-1;T)\leqslant c_2/(c_1-c_2), \quad (25)$$

152

An example of complex scientific calculus typeset in real time display and edited on the Bedford system terminals. Typical of the class of work undetaken by the Composing Room in the 1980s to 2000

Letterpress printing

Letterpress was a relief process initially printing from raised wood carvings and later from metal type and copper halftones to imprint word text and illustrations onto paper.

Letterpress originated in the 1400s using a simple screw design impression press (like a cider press). Letterpress has been the primary printing process in the Western world for making multiple copies of original work. Initially, hand carved wood blocks, with the flat image area highlighted by carving away the surrounding wood, were used to print full pages.

By 1440 Johann Guttenberg had invented movable type and an improved printing press design no longer based on the screw principle. His type consisted of individual wood block letters to compose words. The letters could then be set up and used again and again.

Guttenberg's press still comprised a lower flatbed but the frame mounted top platen was operated through link arms to a pull handle to apply the impression. The linkages could be set up to apply the same weight of impression for each print. The press was more productive than the screw design.

The type was contained in a metal frame known as a chase and locked up with spacers and wedges to secure the type. The locked up pages made up the form which was then inked with a nap leather roller and the paper positioned to lay points on top of the type. Platen pressure then made the print.

Guttenberg's basic printing press design remained in use, with few changes, for 350 years. He improved on wooden type by having type characters cast in metal alloy. This became Founders type, giving a sharper result from longer lasting type. Guttenberg also developed an improved printing ink using lacquer, soot, walnut oil and turpentine.

The first book printed in English in 1473 in Belgium by William Caxton on his improved press is credited with leading to the standardisation of the English language and expansion of the vocabulary.

The first English designed press appeared around 1476 and was a screw design.

Type face designer and gunsmith William Caslon created a clear and distinctive typeface which became widely adopted. Caslon's typeface was used in the printing of the United States Declaration of Independence in 1776.

When William Wheaton undertook his apprenticeship with Honiton printer Spurway in about 1806 the printers' equipment would have consisted only of a platen press, cases of wood type and metal Founders type producing small sheet commercial printing work in the town.

In the eighteenth century, printer John Baskerville created ways to improve the whiteness of paper. He also designed his own typeface which became favoured for bookwork.

By 1850 the invention of the clam shell platen printing press was the first step forward in mechanising the letterpress process. The treadle operated machine cycle involved rollers inking the form on one side of the platen whilst the paper sheet was inserted to lay points by the printer. The clam closed to make the impression. The clam opened and the paper was withdrawn to commence the next impression cycle.

By between 1850 and 1880 small printing businesses had developed in most towns throughout the UK.

From 1880 flatbed hand lever impression platens, such as the Columbian used by Wheatons, were superceded over the years by the clam shell designs.

Early designs of clam shell platen presses originated in the USA and were sold in the UK under license. There were also some UK designs. Most but not all were powered by electric motors after 1900.

In popular use were – Minerva, Arab, Victoria, Phoenix, Sun, Mitre, Invictus, Acme, Furnival and Thompson machines. The Heidelberg Automatic Platen of 1925 became known as the Gilke after a Heidelberg engineer invented the windmill paper feed, impression and printed sheet delivery mechanism. The Heidelberg Platen became one of the basic workhorses of the jobbing printer.

To print larger sheets and improve production speeds, new design stop cylinder machines became available. The Warfdale was one of the first. The form remained locked into a flat steel bed which reciprocated. The form was inked by ink rollers and the paper fed around a cylinder to make the impression.

The 1910–1914 photograph on this page shows Wheatons' first three letterpress cylinder presses (probably Warfdales) and four clam shell platens. All are hand fed but power driven from line shafts.

After the World War II, and by 1950, Wheatons had installed three large Miehle 2 revolution cylinder presses of quad demy size (45 x 50 inch) with automatic paper feeders for book work. The Mielhe would print at about 2,500 sheets per hour. Also installed were four Heidelberg double crown (18 x 24 inch) cylinder presses replacing the platens.

Make ready (the process of getting ready to print the first good copy) could be a lengthy process with letterpress. Each locked up form of type would first be 'scrubbed off' on the back to ensure that no lead filings or other matter were stuck to the surface. All type was cast to a height of 0.918 of an inch. Any impurities on the base of type characters would result

The Letterpress Room in 1910.

The large presses are Wharfedales stop cylinder machines all powered from an overhead drive shaft and belts from the gas engine. A row of Platen presses can be seen on the right of the picture.

Note that all printers and apprentices are 'properly dressed' with starched collars and ties.

By 1935 the company had upgraded the printed presses to electrically powered Miehles printing a sheet of up to 20 inches x 25 inches at 2,500 sheets per hour.

in the character being over height and punching into the paper on impression. Pictures were made as 'blocks' being acid etched from copper sheet by a trade process engraving company. Line drawings were similar but made from zinc sheet. Illustrations were mounted on hardwood blocks cut to the size of the illustration and secured by brads. The total height was 0.918 of an inch, the same as the type. On 'first pull' the printer would judge whether the overall cylinder packing needed adjustment. Otherwise packing thin tissue under the 'tympan' (the top layer of packing which cushioned the impression) may be needed over the half-tone plates to apply more pressure.

All letterpress printers had a dob of paper paste on the back of their left hand for make ready adjustments. A large form could take up to half an hour before an overall dense and evenly printed impression was achieved. There may also be ink roller adjustments required.

The last letterpress machine installed at Fore Street in 1960 was a GMA Tirfing 41 (30 x 40 inches). This Swedish machine could print at up to 3,500 sheets per hour and was probably the fastest flatbed on the market. The press incorporated new features including continuous paper loading and delivery, a stream feeder and built in ink wash up device.

By the 1960s, the development of the flatbed letterpress process, as the primary method of printing, had reached its peak. Rotary letterpress continued, favoured mostly by newspaper publishers to print long runs, but of limited quality. The flatbed letterpress process was renowned for good quality sharp text printing with strong inking and much favoured by book publishers.

One old Victoria platen was retained at Wheatons into the 1960s. The machine was still useful as the impression could be adjusted to accommodate the thickness of a whole book – useful for adding missing text on covers or the first page.

In 1965 the British Federation of Master Printers had 4,000 company members. More than 3,500 of these were mainly letterpress printers. At this time 85% of national printing was still produced by the letterpress process.

The faster litho rotary printing process was developing within the trade but could not yet match the quality and sharpness of letterpress printing. However, litho had the edge on speed of production, shorter make ready times and suitability for illustrated work.

The Letterpress Room in the 1960s. A general view of the depatment shows a range of machines used to print book and commercial work. The main press is a Mieles.

The department included four small Heidelberg cylinder presses for printing book cover (including colour) and commercial work. Small pagination make up sections of four pages and eight pages were also printed on these machines.

In the final years at Fore Street, from 1968, the transition from letterpress to litho began. Bookwork which was expected to reprint was converted to litho by taking high quality 'repro pulls' of text on high grammage art paper or on Barata paper.* The pulls were then photographed to film for plate making and litho printing on the next edition.

However, the changeover was cautiously phased over some six years. Some of the large format letterpress plant and hot metal typesetting keyboards and casters were moved to the new factory in 1973 and continued in use until phased out by 1975 when film setting was introduced.

The litho process, capable of twice the production speed of letterpress, continued to improve with modern printing plates, improved inks and press designs. Litho overtook letterpress in the bookwork field by the late 1970s.

* Barata paper was an expensive substrate sheet with a high quality art paper face, backed with a slightly compressible layer to cushion the print impression. Use of Barata paper gave the ultimate sharp clear print from metal type pages. For best results the printing form on the press had first to be carefully made ready to ensure an overall even impression. This could involve adjusting the thickness of the cylinder under-packing.

Letterpress is not dead. The process is still favoured by small specialist printers supplying quality wedding and event invitations, business cards and private book publications in short runs. The look and feel of the slightly imprinted type, and the strong inking impression on high quality papers and cards gives a superior edge to the product which is still much admired.

Lithography

Lithography is a planigraphic printing process (printing from a level surface image) and based on the principle that oil and water do not mix.

In 1798 Alios Senefelder, a Bavarian playwright, experimented with ways of making copies of his plays for sale. He discovered that script brush writing or drawing on a polished limestone slab in fatty ink made with lamp black, then sponging over with water absorbed by the porous stone but repelled by the ink, prepared a surface for transfer of the image, when under pressure, onto paper. Wetting the stone again, then charging up the ink image, prepared the surface for another print.

By 1817 Senefelder had developed a basic printing press that featured automatic roller damping of the stone and inking of the image area. The press was a flatbed design with geared racks either side of the bed housing the stone. After damping and inking, the paper was placed over the stone and the impression taken by winding a cylinder with carefully set packing over the paper, similar to a mangle, to produce a print.

Initially, the process was favoured by artists to produce prints and posters as it gave far more scope than the alternative letterpress process woodcuts. Using other stones, with other areas of the drawn artwork, colour could be added to the initial mono print. The stones could be cleaned off and used again or stored for reprints.

Printing directly onto the paper from the image on stone was known as direct lithography. A limitation was that abrasive particles in the paper at the time would wear the image, making the process only viable for short runs. Litho stones were heavy and about 3.5 inches (9 cm) thick which limited handling and the size of work printed. Images had to be drawn in reverse.

The next development attributed to Senefelder was the transfer process, whereby drawing right reading (i.e. as you read it) on a special paper with a special ink could be transferred to the litho stone

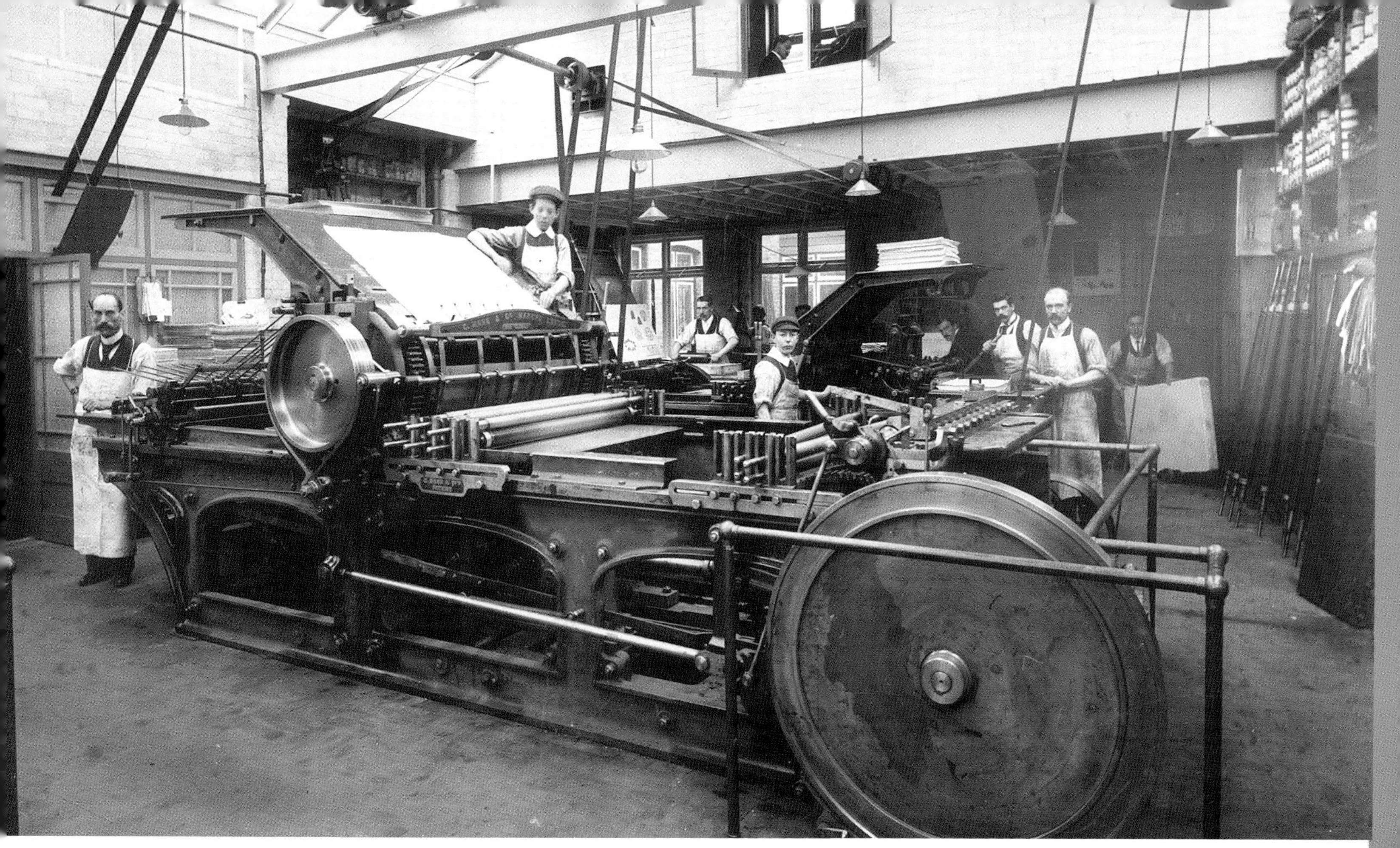

The illustration above shows a George Mann & Co. of Leeds, Climax direct litho press printing from stone in about 1910 at Fore Street. Note the 'fly boy' hand feeding sheets to the lay edge cylinder mounted grippers. The cylinder rotates over the reciprocating bed with the stone to take the impression. The printed sheet is then delivered down tapes to the fly sticks to lay the sheet down in the pile delivery. The damping and ink rollers can be seen. On the right of the picture is a litho stone being manoeuvred. In the background a stone is being inked up by hand using a nappa leather roller – probably for proofing. Power to the press is from overhead pulleys and webbing belts from the gas engine behind the screen on the left. There is no factory heating. The Works Director can be seen in his office above. Production would be at 500–1,000 printed sheets per hour.

under pressure to become a printing image. On impression the printed image on paper became right reading. In addition to artwork, the transfer process enabled composed type printed by letterpress to be transferred to lithography using special inks and transfer paper.

Wheatons were early users of the litho process when the predominant printing method was letterpress.

Lithography remained a slow process due to the flatbed design of the early presses and the weight of the stones for the handlers.

By the 1900s the process had evolved considerably with the development of photography, film and flexible metal plates which could be clamped around a cylinder, leading to the development of the rotary press.

Early experiments to develop a flexible plate concentrated initially on the use of copper but soon zinc was selected as being more suitable. Zinc plates, being soft, could be grained (roughened) on one side to retain moisture during the printing process and key the printing image to the plate. The availability of a flexible plate coupled with developments in photographic processes led to photo lithography enabling half-tone pictures to be included.

Zinc plates were grained using a vibrating trough with the plate at the bottom and a layer of glass marbles roughening the plate surface. The plate was then coated with a light-sensitive solution of egg albumen and gum arabic thinned with water. With the plate inside a circular rotating trough known as a 'whirler', the coating solution was poured onto the plate from the centre by hand using a jug. The revolving action centrifugally distributed the coating evenly out to the edges. The plate was then dried.

Next the plate and negative film text pages were mounted on a clear plastic substrate base and positioned in a vacuum printing-down frame to ensure a sealed contact. The frame was then exposed under powerful open carbon arc lights to transfer and cure the positive image onto the plate. The plate was then washed off to melt away the non-image area coating, then gummed up with gum arabic (a pine tree resin) and dried to prevent oxidation of the zinc.

After use, zinc plates were 'gummed up' and stored hanging on racks available for reprints. Plates would normally be good for up to 60,000 impressions. Often it was cracking of the metal adjacent to the clamps on the printing press cylinders which failed first, rather than a worn image.

These labour-intensive methods of plate making continued at Fore Street until the mid-1960s when the first pre-sensitised aluminium plates became available. Pre-sensitised, coated plates could be taken straight out of the box for printing down from film to plate and so zinc plates were phased out.

The early rotary presses printed directly from the metal plate onto the paper. The abrasive action of contact between the plate and the paper soon caused the image to wear off. Direct rotary litho never became a commercial proposition and was soon succeeded by the offset press.

The offset press removed the direct contact between the plate image and the paper by the addition of a rubber blanket surface. The plate image was transferred to the blanket which in turn was transferred to the paper (or other substrates including metal, e.g. for food cans).

The offset litho press consisted of three cylinders and, as they revolved, the plate cylinder, dampened by rollers, then charged with ink from the ink rollers transferred the image to the blanket cylinder. The paper was introduced between the blanket cylinder and the impression cylinder to transfer the image to the paper. The paper was carried through the press automatically by gripper bars mounted on chains from the paper feeder to the delivery pile enabling a continuous printing process.

Litho presses soon developed to 2-colour designs (effectively two units linked together) and perfectors with a top unit and a lower unit to print both sides of the sheet in one pass.

By the 1920s offset litho presses were gaining ground in the trade due mainly to their suitability to print half-tones and colour more economically and faster than letterpress. Early George Mann offset presses were installed at Fore Street at this time.

The two main British manufacturers of sheetfed offset presses were George Mann and Crabtree, both of Leeds. Wheatons installed two 2-colour Crabtree double demy size presses in about 1930 to print illustrated educational books together with a single colour machine. Later, a Crabtree SP 56 and a Mann NP 56 quad demy size perfector were installed for general book work. Presses would run at 4,000–5,000 sheets per hour.

Over the years the principles of litho have not changed but the technologies developed, significantly overtaking letterpress printing by 1970.

Up to the 1980s plate making involved the use of film, both negative and positive working. Aluminium printing plates available to the trade came pre-sensitised and ready for use. By the late 1970s the 3M company in the USA had developed a waterless litho plate process which was trialled at Wheatons. The 3M plate was tested and used for a year or so but special inks were needed which were expensive. After two years 3M withdrew the product from the market. Waterless plates were later developed by others.

Part of the litho department in the 1940s and 1950s. The machine at the furthest end of the line is the 2-colour Crabtree used by the American Army during World War II.

Pages for plate making were produced initially by photographing typeset pages made up from bromide photographic paper or from customer supplied camera-ready copy (CRC). Film setting machines in the Composing Department later produced page film directly from the Lasercomp typesetting machines.

Negative film had first to be 'spotted'. Negative spotting was the process of painting out with a fine brush and using opaque solution, any minor holes or blemishes in the black non-image area of the negative. The spotting bench was a frosted glass-topped table with back lighting. Spots arose from specks of dust scratches or edge marks which appeared on the CRC or made up bromide pages from the Composing Room. Such marks, if not spotted out, would be printed down to the litho plates and printed with the text.

Spotted negative film was cut to single pages, then hand mounted using red masking tape to clear stable foil sheets

(Astrafoil) laid over ruled-up printing imposition lay sheets on a frosted glass-topped bench illuminated from below. Master imposition layouts were reused for each plate, provided for 8-page, 16-page and 32-page impositions when subsequently printed and folded to sections for binding. The clear margins around the pages were covered by a red light-proof cut out (Rubalith) mask so that only the type areas were clear for exposure to plate. There were a number of additional imposition layouts. Once mounted, the imposed film flat was printed down to plate as previously explained.

The film planning and plate making process was labour intensive. Colourwork involved overlays for each separate colour used in the printing process: cyan, magenta and yellow. The film for each colour was mounted on its own foil and keyed into the black foil. The procedure relied on the accuracy of the planner to sight in for registration using a printer's magnifying glass (linen tester) – known as eyeballing.

Colour registration on the printing press was therefore dependent on the skill of the film planner as the printer could only make minor adjustments on press.

It was the printer's responsibility to double check the work of the film planners. If a mistake had been made it could otherwise go right through subsequent processes and through to the bound book with disastrous consequences.

In the litho and letterpress rooms, on start up, a make-ready sheet would be taken to a ruling-up table with chain drives attached to steel rulers running down and across the table, and used to check the alignment of all rows of all pages. This practice was to ensure that no page was twisted or out of line with others.

Before 'running on' a sheet would be folded up and the front page folio pierced through with a bodkin (awl), then trimmed head, fore edge and foot to the trimmed size of the book. The section was then stapled in the spine margin. A check through page by page would ensure that the bodkin hole pierced all of the folios to confirm page alignment.

The section was then signed off by the printer and the process continued through all sheets in the book. An elastic band retained all of the sections together. The bundle was then passed to the foreman's office and placed in the job bag (works order). When the pallets of printed sheets were delivered to the bindery the foreman could then see that all sections in the book had been accurately printed.

In the 1980s–1990s litho plate making methods changed dramatically proceeding in two stages. At Wheatons a number of advanced new technologies were adopted to reduce the cost of plate making, and improve accuracy and productivity:

3M Pyrofax - enabled typeset pages to be planned up and printed down to electrically charged printing plates. The image area was dusted by the machine with a toner powder which adhered to the type area but not the background (non-image area). This was followed by heat fusing to form a bonded printable image suitable for short run text only work.

The 3M Pyrofax

Opticopy - was a camera page-imposing system working from computer programmes for each imposition layout and exposed to film. The final product was a one-piece film flat for separately printing down to plate. Work was then stored on the system as computer files for reprints. This was suitable for quality work including half-tones.

The Opticopy

Rachwal - was a camera system working from camera-ready pages (CRC) to produce a 70 mm film roll of a book. The film pages were then projected back to print size and automatically printed down to the printing plate, page by page, in a stepping process to designated computer-controlled impositions.

These systems were supplementary to continuing but reducing manual film planning and plate making. They led to the first generation of company staff trained in the use of computers and programming within the print production environment.

By 1990 film imposition was becoming more automated. Input was from customers' own files supplied on disc, or later via the internet or from the company's own typesetting systems. The files were checked on computer screen (pre-flighted) for any missing type fonts or design elements, proofed to the customer if necessary and organised for imposition in the Prepress Studio Department.

For books printed on bulky book wove papers of 80 gsm (grams per square metre) or over, graduated allowances were necessary in the back margins. A folded section would require less spine margin width in the centre compared with the outer pages, with stepped adjustments in between. In this way, fore edge margins of the trimmed pages in sections would be of the same width. The process was known as 'shingling'. Originally allowed for at the hand planning stage, computer plate making systems later accommodated this requirement automatically.

Wheatons brochure promoting their journal production service. The Rachweal Super 70 was the 'first in Europe'.

The second stage of development involved working from computer to large format film and then to plate.

Agfa Avantra direct-to-film systems produced a one-piece plate size film flat of imposed pages under computer control. The film flat was then manually printed down to the printing plate.

Within several years the whole plate making process became automated with the advent of automatically fed VLF and Agfa Excalibur 45 direct-to-plate systems. This took the process one stage further outputting to a final printing plate to ultimate standards of accuracy and definition.

From the 1950s, litho printing presses developed to multi-unit machines with progressively increased automation by the 1980s.

Wheatons' original 2-colour Crabtree presses involved printing a 2-colour sheet twice for 4-colour work. For various reasons registration between the colour of first and second printing were limited. Then, once all sheets were printed on one side they had to be turned and printed on the reverse (backed up). Paper is subject to shrinkage or expansion dependent on weather conditions. Before a sheet was backed up it could be a slightly different size affecting registration between the colours.

Prepared plate damping solutions later included a percentage of alcohol and reduced pure water, leading to sharper print quality. Damping font solution (including approximately 2–3% alcohol) was purchased as a pre-mixed product. As environmental legislation affected the industry, damping solutions became almost alcohol free in favour of chemical damping. Damping rollers, initially covered in cotton stocking, evolved on the Timson ZMR to fine brush damping.

Plate damping required fine control: too much font solution would flood the plate and begin to emulsify with the ink; too little and the plate would 'catch up' with ink invading into the non-image areas and leading to 'scum' on the printed sheet.

In 1967, the Crabtree Sovereign 5-unit colour press from Hillmans was Wheatons' first move into serious colour printing. This perfecting press produced finished colour sheets printed both sides in one pass. However, as with all presses at this time, ink control was by individual multiple turn keys along each of the ink ducts. Make ready involved the printers adjusting these keys to achieve an even fine balance of colour on each unit. On all presses ink was loaded into the ink ducts by pallet knife straight from tins and maintained during the print run. Make ready would take well over an hour, including clamping on printing plates and running up ink adjustments. Start-up paper waste could be considerable.

The Roland 800 4-colour press acquired from Arnolds in 1970 was of the same design era. Presses would run at 4,500 sheets per hour.

Later, Roland and Heidelberg presses became more automated. Computer control of ink ducts via motorised keys and limited adjustment of plate cylinders for fine register were introduced. All controls available to the printer were from a central console and sheet-view table under daylight illumination conditions.

Printing quality was constantly monitored by the printer. A sheet would be pulled out of the delivery at intervals and checked on the bench for registration between colours, scanning colour tabs for ink balance, overall print quality and checking for 'hickies'. These were specks of impurities from the surface of the paper which could build up on the offset blanket cylinder. These would show as small white unprinted specks with a dot in the middle, most noticeably in solid black printed areas. They would require a press stop to wash off the blanket cylinder surface before a restart with resultant start-up paper waste.

The 2011 Man Roland 7–10-unit press went further. This state of the art Hi-Print machine included automatic plate changing between sheets in the job. Ink was automatically pumped from barrels. The printer could control all press functions from the console, including registration, ink and damping balance. Eight printing units produced a perfected colour sheet and the further units were used to provide a seal (varnish) to the printed sheet, preventing marking in the subsequent bindery operations. Powder sprays in the delivery avoided 'set off' between wet sheets in the delivery pile. A further benefit was that printed sheets could soon be forwarded for folding without the previous half-day delay for ink drying. Running speeds increased to 8,000–12,000 sheets per hour.

Wheatons were one of the first UK companies to use web offset litho presses for short run journal and book work.

Web offset, normally the domain of longer-run production, involved the use of paper on reels. The basic principles of the printing press were the same as for sheetfed litho. However, the web press included a folder inline. The end product was folded sections delivered overlapping onto a moving belt.

The format of work produced was limited to the width of the web and the 'cut off' of the folder. The cut off was determined by the circumference of the folder cylinder which, stabilised by pins in the margin area, cut sheets off from the web prior to folding. The folder pulled the paper web through the press from the reel stands.

Therefore, unlike sheetfed printing which can accommodate a range of paper sizes and therefore formats, a web press was limited by design to pre-chosen formats suitable for specific work. Web widths could however be varied to produce some other formats. Paper on reels was mounted on reel stands for either manual unwind (involving stops for splicing the end of one reel to the next) or automatic splicing without stops. Web presses were at least twice as fast as sheetfed machines.

Wheatons' first move from sheetfed printing into web offset printing came after the company was acquired by Pergamon Press in 1966.

Pergamon's scientific journals programme of 360 titles was printed by a number of UK companies around the country in runs of 1,000 to 3,000 copies, published monthly, bi-monthly and quarterly. A number of different formats and papers were used.

In 1972 Anthony Wheaton presented a proposal to the Pergamon Board showing that by using small web offset presses and just two standard formats and two standard papers, considerable economies could be made in production costs. The report detailed the value of projected savings over the following five years and well justified the proposal. The plan would be backed by a phased build up of Group journals placed with Wheatons.

The last of the three Cottrell Marinoni web presses before being replaced by more modern machines

The plan was approved. However it took nearly two years for the Publishing Division to cautiously convince the journal editors, who held considerable sway, to change their long-established formats and style.

The production approach was to print the journals on web offset presses in batches of five to ten titles at a time which made web offset viable even for short runs. The presses would remain set up for the next batch, thus saving almost all of previous make ready costs and paper waste incurred when printing one job at a time by sheetfed litho. Changing the printing plates on the web presses was achieved in just 6 minutes. In addition, paper purchased on reels was 10–15% cheaper than sheet paper.

Installed in 1973, Wheatons' first two web offset presses were a Cottrell Marinoni N420A A4 format and a N420B 275 mm x 160 mm format, cold set single unit machines with manual reel stands producing 16-page folded sections.

The batch production approach proved very cost effective. Over the next few years and by 1978, the journals programme at Exeter increased to 160 titles, along with some academic book work suitable for the fixed formats.

By 1985 the company had added a Harris N420D A4 2-unit web press producing 32-page sections mono or 16-page in 2-colours. Later, a further Harris 4-unit press was installed for 32-page 2-colour catalogue work. A Solna 4-colour heat set web and a Timson T 32 book press, which were elderly but useful machines, were brought in from other companies in the Group.

The 2004 Timson ZMR mono and 2-colour heat set press was the most advanced design and technology for batch production of journals and printing of large page extent directories and catalogues. It was capable of running mono work non-stop by printing from one perfecting unit whilst the second unit was automatically plated up for the next section. The press would reciprocate printing from each unit until all sections in the job were completed at a constant speed of up to 18,000 folded and bundled sections per hour.

The cold set Harris web presses were limited to printing on relatively soft papers to ensure that the ink had time to absorb enough to avoid marking in the press folder. In contrast, the Timson ZMR was a heat set press and enabled printing without drying problems on smooth papers, matt-coated cartridges, etc. required for catalogues and commercial publications. The press was also capable of printing on lightweight papers down to 30 gsm.

Paper tension had to be carefully controlled on web offset presses. On the early Harris presses, tension was provided by a light braking action applied from the manual reel stands to prevent overrun of the paper web as the press was slowed down to a stop. On the Timson, the web tension was controlled from the automatic reel splicing reel stands.

Too much tension, or over damping of the printing plates before start up, could cause web breaks. Web breaks would involve the time consuming process of re-threading the web through the press units, the dryers and web support rollers through to the folder.

Web splicing (joining one reel to the next) on manual unwind reel stands, as on the Cottrell Marinoni and Harris machines, the press had to be stopped to make the splice with double-sided adhesive tape between the nearly used reel and the next full reel. The printed section with the splice included would be subsequently removed from the folder delivery belt on start up.

The Timson ZMR was equipped with automatic reel splicing units. The next to run reels were pre-prepared with double-sided tape applied. On a pre-set minimum on the reel core of the current web being printed the machine would automatically make the splice on computer command.

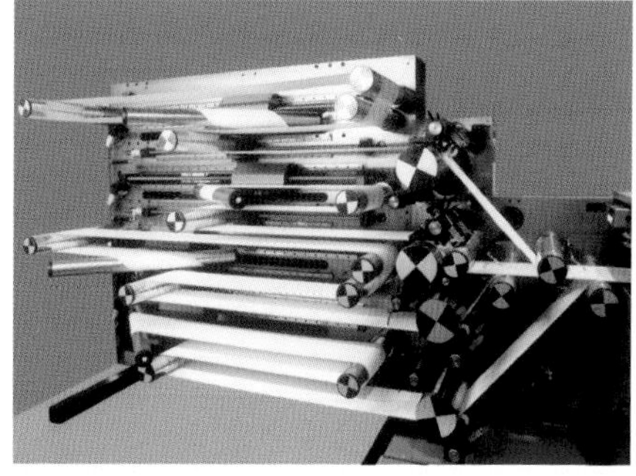

2005/2006 *The Timson T48 ZMR 2-Unit, non-stop (zero make-ready) heat set web offset press – an overview of the installation at Wheatons*

Bottom left and above right: *Showroom pictures of the T48 show printing units, web divert unit and the folder. The close up of the divert unit shows how the printed web was split into parallel ribbons and then diverted by rollers to form one merged ribbon feeding into the folder.*

The splicer mechanism included a buffer of web length festooned between 'dancer' rollers. Whilst the web continued running from the few seconds of paper length from the buffer, the next paper reel would swing over to contact the current reel and join on the next web. At the same time a cutting knife would part off the nearly expired first reel. There would be no slowing down of the press for a reel change.

Changing from one type of paper to another was achieved by leaving a tail of the previous paper through the press. The new paper was spliced onto this tail with double-sided tape and then run slowly through the press to the folder.

All web press folders basically produced fixed formats but there could be some variation by running narrower reels. Formats can be varied in one direction but the 'cut off' of the folder would be constant. This would produce excess paper in one margin direction and would be 'cut to waste' in the bindery as the book block was trimmed to final format size.

Varying reel widths were not ideal practice. If smaller reels were run regularly, the cylinder rubber blankets became compressed along the edge of the narrower web to give rise to 'tramlines'. The slight difference in printing impression could be noticeable on the printed work. This practice would lead to the need to change blankets more frequently.

On the Timson ZMR, after running through the dryers, the paper web became crisp. To re-condition the paper, the web was re-moisturised by fine water sprays to bring the paper back to its original form and to aid folding. Over moisturising could produce 'cockling', an undesirable wavy condition which may remain apparent in the finished trimmed book.

Wheatons' web presses were equipped with two folding options – quarter-fold (for journals and directory formats) and double parallel (for small publications and books). Quarter-fold produced a single A4 section. Double parallel was used for smaller A5 formats printed two-up – one section above another. The two sections remained attached through binding to the final book trimming stage producing two books at a time. Alternatively, two different sections of the same book could be printed two-up and then split in half in the bindery, prior to section gathering.

All papers have a grain direction arising from the laydown of the wood pulp and fibres on the Fourdrinier design papermaking machines. On Wheatons' web presses the grain would run head-to-foot on an A4 quarter-fold, and spine to fore edge on A5 double parallel folds. Grain direction slightly affects the lay of pages when a book is in use.

After printing the web ran over a ^ formation former (known as a kite) to fold the running web in half before entering the folder. As cross folds were made, particularly on heavier papers, trapped air was a problem which at speed could produce creasing in head folds known as 'crow's feet'. This problem could usually be avoided by running perforation disks to partially split the head fold to enable the air to escape.

On the Timson ZMR a far more advanced and versatile solution was incorporated. Before the printed web reached the folder it entered a divert unit. This equipment split the running web into parallel ribbons from one to four depending on format and section pagination requirements. The ribbons were guided by rollers to form a single super imposed ribbon before cross folding. The open edges of the sections released all air and eliminated creasing. The ZMR folder could produce a variety of paginations – A4 48 pages, A5 64 pages and A6 64 pages. Also, A4 48 pages could be split to produce 24-page sections. The divert unit enabled papers down to 29 gsm (Bible weight) to be printed on the press.

The folded book sections were delivered from the folder onto a moving delivery belt which fed directly into the bundling unit. The bundler collected pre-set quantities of sections, compressed them and strapped them in bundles to produce 'logs' for handling. When all sections in the book were printed and bundled with individual section identification added in an assembly area, the order was ready for the bindery.

At Sheffield, Polestar's 2015-installed Goss 96-page Sunday 5,000 presses were the worldwide ultimate in web press design and control technologies. The presses ran webs of 2.860 metres wide, printing to the highest standards possible in full colour perfected webs, delivering as split ribbons into three PcF3 pinless folders. Each ribbon was either the next sections in the title or a separate title running together with the first. New engineering design features included removable sleeve cylinders (no rubber blankets) and gapless plate cylinders. These features and others enabled production press speeds of 60,000 impressions per hour (iph) or more.

The first two presses were successfully commissioned for production in early 2016. Ironically, among the last orders to be printed before the Receiver closed the plant by 31 May, was an edition of the *TV Radio Times*. The contract with the BBC had been retained through the BPCC and Polestar years after the heroic contribution by Wheatons' typesetters in 1983–84 in maintaining the contract.

Given more time, Polestar's plan may well have succeeded.

Digital production

Since 2000, the market for published information, previously the domain of print, has not reduced but it has shifted towards new technology solutions for shorter run work.

Due to the high start up costs of printed work, including making printing plates, a reasonable print run was necessary to spread these costs over the job. The more copies produced the cheaper each became. This in turn meant that publishers and commercial customers often ordered more that they required to obtain a lower unit price. They then had costs associated with warehousing the stock and there could be waste as unused product.

Digital production from customer files supplied as PDFs (portable document format*), only involved checking the files and organising the work for stream feeding to digital production systems. The cost of printing plates, press set ups and start-up paper waste associated with conventional printing was largely eliminated. The customer could order small quantities and top up on demand at much the same unit price as the first order. Stockholding costs were much reduced. The quality of digital was acceptable in most markets but for colour digital the range of papers was more restricted.

Personalised product promotions and mailings were a good example of the flexibility of digital production. Each individual copy could be different from the

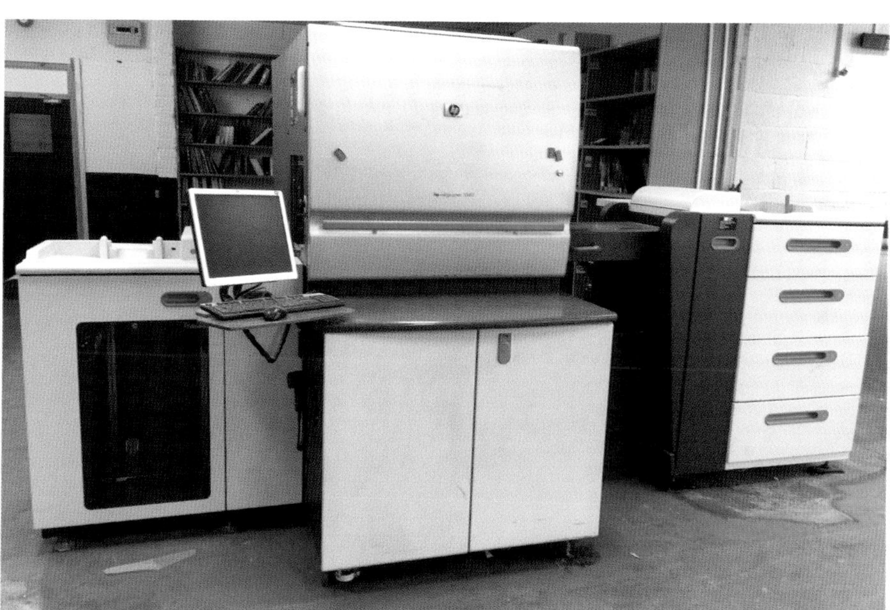

With the HP 7250 high speed colour web and HP Indigo 5,500 (shown above),the Digital Department was well equipped for variable data digital production and short run journal and book printing.

The illustrations show the HP 5,500 high quality sheet fed digital system and the imaging heads withdrawn on the HP colour web system.

* **PDF**. Developed by Adobe Systems, a PDF is a Portable Document File extension. PDFs do not rely on the software that created them or any specific operating system or hardware. They are a secure way of sending graphics and text work documents between locations without risk of corruption.

Examples of digitally produced short run books.

one before and different from the next. Also, the next order could be seamlessly fed to the digital imaging equipment without waste or delay.

Digital imaging equipment using toner ink from graphic design transfers was widely used for vehicles, large format posters, leaflets and brochures, mailings, booklets and journals, etc.

Digital production for books involved flowline equipment from imaging to the bindery. Book print on demand (POD) services enabled orders from one copy to a few hundred to be produced at low cost.

By 2010 inkjet technology (involving droplets to make up the image) supplemented digital toner-based technology. Initially inkjet was a low definition process used for marking products, labels and packages, etc. but as sharpness of imagery improved, the process came into wider use including text publications.

Timpson Engineering succeeded in developing its T-Press, launched in 2012 as a digitally driven 'printing' press for book work, but could not sustain production due to insufficient orders at the time.

The digital market continued to grow at the expense of conventional litho printing. Printing looked set to decline slowly but remained relevant for longer run publications. Directories, catalogues and lists continued at a lower level, often alongside online versions of the same publications.

By 2015 an even newer technology was emerging, based on nanotechnology, which involved computer driven manipulation of matter (ink) on a molecular scale.

Over 500 years the letterpress process had remained the principal method of distributing the printed word. However, just the past 50 years have seen huge steps forward. Letterpress was replaced by lithography in the1960s, then the introduction of fax machines, high quality laser printers, digital 'printing' systems and inkjet technology followed. Now nanography seemed set to be the way forward in selected market niches.

Digital production equipment was relatively lightweight in engineering terms and involved high maintenance costs. The process was best suited for short runs and testing markets. The versatility and flexibility at low cost in addressing market sectors were the advantages of digital, working from PDF files supplied over the internet by customers anywhere in the world.

Book binding

Book binding was a well developed craft 200 years ago. Most books were elaborately hand-bound using leather skivers (split, cured layers of animal skin) for cases which were then intricately hand tooled using fillets and rolls to apply gold leaf and other colour foils. Wording was blocked onto the case by heated impression from brass type. The hand sewn book sections were over-casted to provide ridges on the spine. The trimmed sewn book blocks would have marble patterning applied to the head and perhaps other edges.

There is no record of Wheatons practising such skills. The surviving copy of the 1846 Wheaton Almanack is unfortunately unbound but would have been section sewn, probably with a limp cover. Much of the general printing work from William Wheaton's small printing business behind the bookshop would have been handbills, folded leaflets or stitched self-cover products. Any special hard case binding requirement may have been outworked to a craft bookbinder.

The first Wheatons' educational books were single section wire-stitched booklets with pull over covers. In 1927 Fred Wheaton and his Works Manager, Mr Hutt, travelled to London to purchase hard case binding equipment from a printer who was closing down.

The plant included a Smyth-Horne case-making machine and a book-casing-in machine, together with a Crawley rounder and backer. Also added was a Bury book press with brass, raised edge book pressing boards and a Curtis air compressor to operate the press.

Cased-in bound books would be laid out around the edges of each board with the brass raised lips pressing into the spine grooves. Boards with books would be loaded up to a height of about 6 feet in the manner of a cider press. The books would remain under pressure overnight until dry.

The bindery foreman at the time was a Mr Powell who, on his own initiative, began experimenting in making corrugated cardboard boxes *(see advert on page 18)*. This activity became a very successful side-line and supplied local businesses at a time when there was no competition in Exeter. The boxes were printed with the name and address of the customer and were made to a minimum order of 500 units. They were supplied to outfitters, ladies' dress shops, milliners, laundries and grocers. The boxes would be cut out in the flat form from a standard range of designs and then stored. The customer would then call off a quantity which would be assembled, stapled up and delivered within 12 hours, guaranteed.

Additional book binding equipment was acquired to include a Greig book spine smasher, section sewing machines, Brehmer, Cundall & Camco printed sheet folding machines, a Rosback book spine lining machine and a three-knife book block trimmer. There was no section collating machine acquired. In the 1930s Wheatons' educational books and other publishers' titles were of relatively low pagination. The first method to collate

sections for a book consisted of laying piles out in order around a large table, then collating these by walking around the table taking one section from each pile to collate a book.

This method was soon 'mechanised'. The Maintenance Department designed and built a circular table of 8 feet or so in diameter and mounted it on half a back axle of a car where the wheel would have normally been attached. The differential gears were utilised to give a right angle drive and gear reduction to an electric motor to provide a controllable rotating table. Up to eight bindery staff sitting on chairs could be accommodated around the table. The 'leader' controlled the start-stop by a foot pedal. Piles of numbered sections were placed around the table. As the table slowly revolved, each person picked up a section. One revolution represented eight books collated to full pagination up to 256 pages.

Large printed sheets from the machine rooms were delivered on pallets to the bindery. The sheets were machine folded to the various page imposition configurations often involving slitting the sheets on the folder to provide two

Left: *Bookbinders tools for applying foils*

1935 Bookbinding machinery at Fore Street

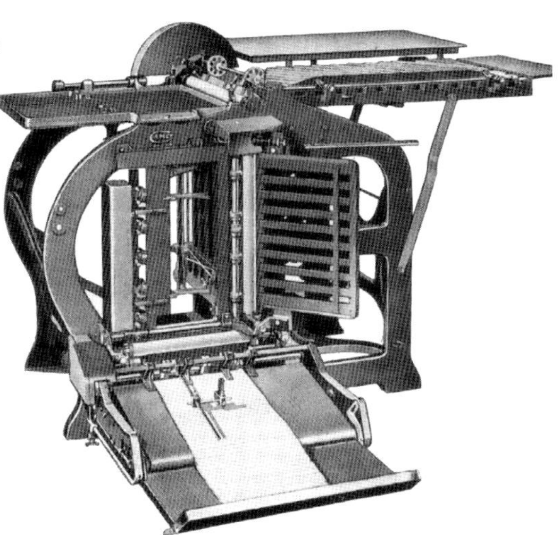

AMC buckle sheet folder

Smythe Horne '3 wing' book casing-in machine

Smythe-Horne book case-making machine

Single knife guillotine

32-page or four 16-page, etc. folded sections to a sheet. The imposition laydowns were industry-standard coded and used by the planners in litho plate making or the Composing Department stone room (when type metal pages were still in use).

When collating sections in the bindery to produce book paginations, it was vitally important to check that all folded sections were in numerical page order (although at this stage folded sections could not be opened to check this). To facilitate checking, a printed spine code ladder system was used. This involved a 15 x 2 mm solid tab printed in the outer spine fold. The tab position would be stepped down a notch for each section in the book. The bottom of the first tab lined up with the top of the next. Looking at the back of a collated set of sections, the stepped tabs would immediately indicate if one was out of position, meaning a section was in the wrong place. For sewn books the section sewing operator would check these tabs before sewing sections together to form an untrimmed book block. Hard case binding commenced at Fore Street in late 1927, giving the company the facility to produce professionally presented books for the home and overseas markets.

For durability school books were usually thread sewn or wire stitched. Pamphlet-style books could also be Singer sewn which involved a continuous run of stitches through the length of the spine centrefold to ensure that pages could not be pulled out.

The next development, as the company also moved into binding for general publishers' work, was the acquisition of a Martini Pony binder for hotmelt glue binding of square-backed flexi-cover books. This machine was purchased secondhand from the Hotspur Press in Manchester in about 1965.

The new bindery, of 25,000 square feet, was opened in 1968 and was the first phase of the Marsh Barton factory development. Soon after an adjacent 25,000 square feet warehouse was added.

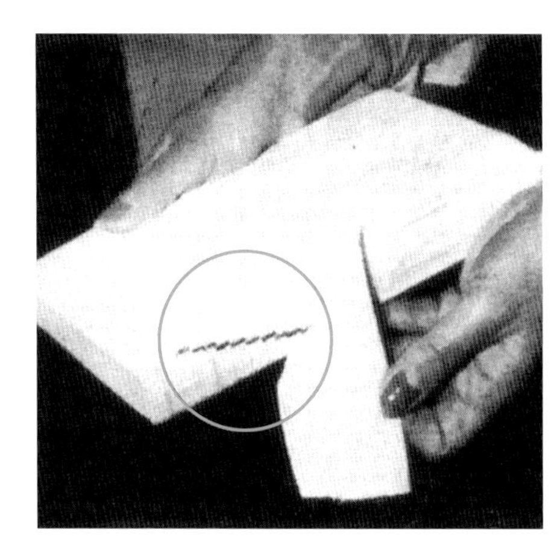

Spine tabs indicate at a glance that all sections in a book are correctly collated before sewing.

More modern plant was acquired to include a Martini stitching line to gather up and wire stitch up to 96-page plus cover publications. A Martini unsewn PVA-glue cold set binding machine and a Martini Norm unsewn hotmelt binding line were a higher capacity replacement for the Pony binder. A Kolbus 36-books-per-minute binding line for hard case books and additional three-knife trimmers completed the upgrades. The Rosback spine lining machine was retained as a useful backup and for other work.

As the company's book production services developed, machine collating commenced with a Martini hopper-fed collator for hard case books.

The machine comprised mechanical hopper section feeders delivering onto a belt. Each section on pre-organised pallets was located by each hopper. The page extent of the book determined how many hoppers would be required. An operator could manage two hoppers and when the machine started would keep the hoppers topped up. Upstanding notches on the belt propelled the sections along as each section dropped on top of the one before. At the end of the collation the set of sections making up the book was assembled ready for sewing.

For hard case binding, front and back sections would require 4-page folded end papers to be tipped on before collating. The end papers would later be pasted down to the inside of the book cases to help unit the book block with the hard cover.

Hard case books would be brought up to the sewn book block stage, then trimmed head and foot and fore edge to required final book size. They would then be run through the Kolbus line for rounding and backing of the spine to create shoulders or left flat if for a square-back style. The spines would then be glued and lined in one or two linings. One lining was a 'crash' open weave material which would be some 3 cm wider on both sides of the book block spine to adhere the book together with the end papers into the case, on casing-in and pressing.

1980s Mechanical section gathering

For limp bound (flexi-cover) book binding two Martini combined collating and binding production lines were installed in the 1970s. These combined collating from hopper feeders and completed the binding in one flowline integrated operation.

Unsewn perfect bound books required the folded spines on sections to be milled off to clear the folds and expose all individual pages, prior to the spine glue application. This was allowed for at the plate making stage by adding an allowance of 6 mm to all spine fold 'gutter' positions. When the sheet was folded to sections this provided 3 mm for spine-milling allowance. Thicker papers may have required more.

Wire-stitched binding of small jobs was undertaken on a saddle stitching machine with two or three wiring heads. Sections were placed by hand on a ^ shaped saddle. Depending on pagination up to three or so sections and a cover could be placed on top of each other prior to stitching to form a booklet or a magazine.

For longer wire-stitched runs, a Martini gang stitcher worked in the same manner but with hoppers feeding sections onto a chain running throughout the length of the

Kolbus hard cased binding line

machine. The chain brought the sections and a cover to the stitching heads in a continuous operation which was followed by trimming to final size.

The Kolbus line combined previously individual operations of spine rounding and backing, two spine linings and book block casing-in and pressing, all in one pass.

More modern Stahl and MBO knife and buckle printed sheet folding machines replaced the smaller of the old folders. Wohlenberg programmatic guillotines replaced older Kraus machines. By the 1990s a Martini Monoblock hotmelt binding line with a 12-station section gatherer complemented the Norm binder. Sitma individual plastic packing and labelling equipment was added for mailing requirements.

During the 1980s the UK book production market was declining. It was considered that hard case binding would give way to flexi-cover binding on economic grounds. For a period of several years the bindery was cut back and the Kolbus hard case line was removed. As the company's publisher customers frequently required a small hard case run of an otherwise flexi-cover edition, the company was at a disadvantage. To address this, a Smyth three-wing casing-in machine was reinstated so that a limited hard case service could be maintained. Later, as the company refocused on editions requiring hard case binding, the Kolbus line was brought back.

In 1988, BPCC considered closing the Exeter bindery and concentrating all binding work at other Group plants suffering from the falling book market. After debate this idea was recognised as an illogical option as Wheatons would be unable to offer a necessary complete service to book publishers from one site. Also, fortunately, there were logistical considerations in favour of leaving binding at Wheatons.

In 2004 the Martini Bolero PUR glue binding line was the state of the art machine and the first to be installed in the UK. The Bolero replaced the two older Martini lines. The Bolero involved computer set ups for each job and could be programmed to set up the next job whilst the current job was still running. Binding at 4,000 books per hour for A4 quarter fold formats and 8,000 books per hour from two-up smaller format sections, the binding line was far more productive than earlier plant. With 27 section feeding stations, publications of up to 1,200 pages could be collated and bound in one pass

The Muller Martini binding line

without the need to pre-collate sections.

PUR (polyurethane reactive adhesive) gave far superior binding strength and longevity compared with previous hotmelt or PVA adhesives. With a page pull rating 40–50% stronger than hotmelt it was the ultimate glue technology for heavy catalogues which would need to withstand rigorous use.

After binding, the books as single or two-up copies, now with covers applied, were delivered onto a spiral moving belt system. This allowed 20 to 30 seconds for the glue to set before entering the three-knife trimming machine to produce the final format books.

All trimming waste was vacuum sucked away through a trunking system to a waste baling plant running at the same time as the binder.

The company logos throughout the years

The first Wheaton Print Company logo 1900 – 1905. Wheat-on-XTR. (Wheaton Exeter). Wheaton Exeter Limited –Booksellers, Publishers and Printers.

This logo was used by the Educational Publishing Department in the late 1950s.

New logos for the companies letterheads:
Left: for the printing departments.
Right: for the Schools Supplies Departments.

This logo was used by the Publishing Department during the late 60s.

The Pergamon logo. Pergamon was an ancient Greek city. The colophon is a reproduction from a coin dating from about 400 BC, showing the head of the goddess of Athens.

This logo was used by the Publishing Department during the early 70s.

This logo was used by the Printing Department during the early 70s.

This logo was used by the Printing Department during the early 80s.

The logo of the British Printing and Communications Corporation (BPCC) was designed in 1987 by the marketing department then housed at the *Mirror* building. The logo is designed around the concept of group web offset printing activity.

Both the Devon Books and Arnold Wheaton logos belonged to the publishing side of the company. Arnold Wheaton was the combination of the two group companies, Wheaton Publishers, Exeter and E J Arnold of Leeds.

The Polestar Group logo from 1998. Each group member featured its company name.

The Polestar logo derives from the 'O' featured in cyan symbolising the world, with the North Star hovering above.

The final logo used by the company ironically turned out to be a revision of the very first. The new management updated the circular type to read 'Web Offset and Lithographic Printers'.

Tail Piece

Although faced with the difficulties of working in a declining market, Wheatons operated profitably until later years but never fitted comfortably within a large commercial print manufacturing group.

The Polestar culture was not sufficiently tuned to the needs of smaller publishers and the academic and educational markets which were Wheatons' mainstay. It could be observed that successive managing directors, transferred from Polestar companies for short periods, could not provide continuity, stability and directional planning for the future.

If Robert Maxwell had been content with scientific and academic publishing and not seized the opportunity to acquire bankrupt BPC which he knew would bring high profile publicity and entry into media publishing and production – it could all have been so different. Perhaps he got a taste for printing, the smell of the ink, the sound of production and the unions at Wheatons after 1966. Even prior to that, it was Anthony Wheaton who opened the account with Pergamon Press in 1965 after an introduction from Cecil Jeans, Sales Director of Santype Salisbury, who were technical typesetters to Pergamon.

Perhaps not ideal but nonetheless, who else but Pergamon Press would have put up the funds for the new factory and new plant investments in 1966? And again, in 2014, if not Polestar, who else would have funded Wheatons' substantial deficits for three years after the loss of the Elsevier journals whilst in financial difficulties themselves?

There are many stories which could be told about working with Robert Maxwell and others – sufficient to fill another book!

The changing needs of publishers and other customers, the digital world, free trade, the internet, rapid advances in technology and automated equipment had all contributed to the loss of conventional trade skills and the decline in the book production trade.

By 2012, at the time of the loss of the Elsevier journals contract, the Digital Department was well developed and equipped with services to meet the needs of the evolving markets for short run publications and variable data work including mailing solutions.

However, five years before the MBO, Polestar were unable to commit the further investment needed to keep up with the fast-developing digital markets. Further services to meet the needs of self-publishers, print on demand, versatile digital promotional services and IT solutions, and stock fulfilment could not be addressed. Such services alongside conventional print would have given the company a higher market profile and time to adjust to the decline in the conventional market.

Maxwell's Way
Negotiating with Unions

In 1966, Wheatons was Robert Maxwell's first significant acquisition of a UK printing company. In the years that followed he had his introductions to negotiating with the UK print unions. The unions could be intransigent to change and resisted measures which would affect their members as the company sought to reduce operating costs.

The late Robert Maxwell

By the late 1970s, UK manufacturing industries generally became progressively less competitive in international markets under the then Labour government. High national inflation was driving up wage claims and production material costs – actions had to be taken to keep the company viable.

Frustrated by the time wasted in traditional negotiations with the unions, Maxwell began developing his own approach and style.

The following extract from the *The Way of the Sun* well describes Maxwell's tactics which were further honed during the 1980s and would be instantly recognisable to Wheaton's managers and FOCs.

Article

The Way of the Sun is the story of Sun Engraving Company, Sun Printers and Odhams in Watford – major BPCC companies before their final closure in 2004. Published in 2010, the 380 page book was printed by Polestar Wheatons – the only remaining book printing company in the Group.

See pages 182 – 183 for extract.

From the book *The Way of the Sun*

by Peter Greenhill and Brian Reynolds

Taken from Chapter 20, pages 222–224: ***'The Impact of Robert Maxwell'***

As one of the largest companies in BPC, the Sun became the subject of Maxwell's personal attention during the survival plan negotiations. He visited the plant frequently and there were more visits by Sun management and trade union officials to his offices in Worship House (later, Maxwell House) in London.

The survival plan was negotiated in remarkably short order. Gone at last, it seemed, were the days of endless wrangling followed by the inevitable grubby compromises. Maxwell appeared, at first, to be giving the unions their way, surrendering many management proposals and causing serious irritation in the upper ranks. But he was working to his own agenda, first mollifying and then ensnaring the chapel officials so that management would get what it wanted in the end. One concession the directors were particularly eager to have was an end to full-time chapel officials, but that objective took a couple of years to achieve, not least because Maxwell saw these officials as useful to him in the early days. He showered them with attention, flattered them and made them feel important. On one memorable occasion, knowing that Bill Ford was vacationing at a holiday camp, he sent a helicopter to the camp to collect him and bring him back to a meeting. The prestige that attached to such treatment made lapdogs of FOCs – and got Ford, for instance, so firmly on Maxwell's side that he would then work to sway other chapel representatives. In his efforts to obtain swift agreement, Maxwell would also call mass meetings of the workforce and address the rank and file directly. By doing so, he appeared to be bypassing Sun management, but he was also circumventing the usual filtering of management's words by FOCs, and ensuring that the shop floor heard the message straight from the horse's mouth.

Even then, smooth sailing wasn't guaranteed. In mid-March the survival plan talks were nearly derailed when composing room employees refused to do overtime work at the management's request. They were immediately suspended, apparently on Maxwell's orders. The suspension was lifted three hours later when the men agreed to participate in further talks and to work a certain amount of extra time.

Maxwell's involvement was surely a factor in the issue's quick resolution. The threat of closure was never far from his lips. He made clear during negotiations that he owned the company and that it was his to do with as he wished. He had the power and personality to carry out his threats, and the unions soon realized that their usual fallback tactics of slowdowns and strike threats wouldn't work with him and might even backfire.

He had no compunction about intervening at whatever level would give him what he wanted. He had built close relationships with the national and regional leaders of the printing unions, who clearly found him hard to resist. He seduced them by praising them publicly, but they also knew that he invested in his companies and that he didn't just demand redundancies; he also created jobs. Nor could they ignore the fact that, like Rupert Murdoch, he had the power of sole ownership and was fully prepared to use it.

Maxwell met with national union officials behind the scenes and obtained their broad prior agreement to the Sun's survival plan. It is doubtful that they felt undue concern for their Sun Printers members, whose wage rates and other benefits were well in excess of those of the majority of their members (many of whom were also employed by Maxwell). The Sun's chapel representatives were less realistic and can never have been said to have had the company's long-term interests at heart. For the time being, however, they proved relatively cooperative.

The survival plan that took shape contained clauses that, in the previous decade, would have sent the workforce into the streets. It called for a significant reduction in manpower (some 400 workers) through voluntary redundancies, the introduction of compulsory retirement at sixty-five, and elimination of many formerly untouchable restrictive practices.

Eventually, every chapel, except that of the Amalgamated Engineering Union, accepted and signed the plan. But Maxwell had insisted that *all* chapels must agree and sign, or the plan would fail. At a meeting in Watford involving Maxwell, Brian Reynolds, David Staton, and the AEU chapel, FOC Bill Lloyd expressed his members' concern – a matter of lack of trust in Maxwell. Maxwell listened intently, then responded by blaming the two directors at the table for having "misled" him as to the chapel's reason for refusing to sign. With his right hand pressed to his heart, he said that he had been deeply hurt upon hearing that the chapel didn't trust him. He asked that they give the survival plan a chance for six months, after which time they could raise any outstanding concerns directly with him and he would review the situation directly with them. At that, the final signature was put on the plan and there were handshakes all round.

Once the AEU officials had left, the two directors took Maxwell to task over his false accusation. His response was typically oblique, and only tangentially related to the discussion that was actually taking place. "Don't worry about that," he replied. "I spoke to their national officials this morning and told them the consequences of the local chapel not signing. They won't cause any problems."

Becoming familiar with Maxwell's *modus operandi* made it a little easier for senior management to accept the public criticism he sometimes unfairly bestowed on them. It was all part of his act. He would tell the shop floor: "The board has let you down and I'm here to save things," and would get what he wanted from the rank and file. "He was a very intelligent animal," recalls Fred Frost, "but entirely without principles."

On the April day in 1981 when the Sun's survival plan was formally signed and sealed, photographs were taken in the boardroom and outside the Sun's main entrance. They show Maxwell joking and being chummy with various smiling FOCs. Perhaps everyone believed that the worst was over.

With his conditions met, Maxwell delivered the promised £10 million to BPC. In doing so, he increased his holdings to 77 per cent and took control of the corporation. ■

The Way of the Sun is published by True to Type Books (2010), Claremont, Ontario, Canada. ISBN 978-0-9866167-0-9.

Sources

This book has been compiled from archival informations and illustrations in the possession of the author together with further material contributed by others. The dates of some appointments and events may be approximate.

The author has made every attempt to locate owners of copyright material or to acknowledge such material but would be grateful for any information which would allow the correction of any errors in any subsequent edition of this work.

A commemorative mug was given to staff, guests and clients on the celebration of the completion of the Marsh Barton factory. The mug featured the Greig–Columbian platen press that stood in the stairwell of the main entrance for many years.

Magazine articles

Printweek (incorporating Lithoweek) & Printing World – www.printweek.com

05.08 2004 Non-stop press to Exeter
04.04.2013 Polestar to revamp press halls
24.03.2016 Polestar pre-pack confirmed
24.05.2016 End of the Line for Polestar, Sheffield
25.05.2016 Polestar goes into administration
13.06.2016 Polestar Stones/Wheatons buyout confirmed
13.07.2016 Administrators detail Polestar sales
08.01.2017 Polestar time-line – Will the promise of jam tomorrow ever be delivered?

Classic Motorcycle Magazine: Mortons Archive – wwwmortonsarchive.com

Newspaper Articles

The Guardian
27.04.2016 UK's largest independent printer – Polestar calls in the Administrators

Express & Echo, Exeter – www.exeterexpressandecho.co.uk

Publications

Exeter Memoirs – www.exetermemoirs.co.uk
The Exeter Floods of the 1960s
The Exeter Blitz April May 1942
The Way of the Sun – The Story of Sun Engraving and Sun Printers. Published by True Type Books.